Stenographers to Power

Media and Propaganda

David Barsamian

Common Courage Press   Monroe, Maine

ISBN: 0-9628838-4-0 paper

ISBN: 0-9628838-5-9 cloth

Common Courage Press
P.O. Box 702
Monroe, ME 04951
207-525-0900

Second Printing

For my father
Bedros Barsamian,
"Hairig"

Contents

III. Examples

IV. Defense against Thought Control

Introduction:
Resisting Thought Control

The popular cultural representation of the U.S. media is that they are adversarial to, and independent of, state and corporate power. This well cultivated and consciously promoted image quickly dissolves under the lens of scrutiny.

The actual purpose which the media serve very effectively is to inculcate and defend the economic, social and political agenda of privileged groups that dominate domestic society and state. Myriad techniques are employed including: selection of topics, distribution of concerns, framing of issues, story placement, filtering of information, emphasis and tone, Orwellisms, photographs, etc. The media inoculate the public against reality creating a *cordon sanitaire* between fact and fiction. History and context, if not ignored is distorted. Thus, Iraq invades Kuwait. War happens. It breaks out like measles or smallpox. No background is offered. The Gulf War is a textbook example of "nuzak" where journalists were virtually indistinguishable from stenographers.

The reasons for this pattern are clear. The media are corporations that have a market: other businesses that advertise through the media. The media are selling their advertisers a product, namely readers and audiences. From an institutional point of view that is what the corporate media are: enterprises out to make money, like other businesses. Their behavior is rational. They reflect the interests of their owners. The media are a tool for constraining political debate within limits that serve the interests of the ruling elite by controlling our understanding of what is politically possible.

1

The interviews in this book deconstruct the assumptions and premises of the mainstream media which reflect their owners' interests, and suggest other approaches.

Alternative media are hindered and marginalized by lack of resources. Nevertheless, in recent years new media have developed such as *Z* magazine, South End Press, *Lies of Our Times*, and *Extra*. Numerous community radio stations and cable access contribute much to increasing political participation and pluralism.

KGNU radio in Boulder, Colorado, began in 1978 is a case in point. The station broadcasts dissident views and provides a public forum for direct community participation. It was at KGNU that I began to develop my own broadcasting and interviewing skills.

Thanks to all the interviewees in this book and elsewhere who have allowed me to come into their lives with tape and microphone. Special thanks to Sandy Adler for her invaluable assistance. And thanks also too to Greg Bates, a patient and persistent editor.

David Barsamian
Boulder, Colorado
October, 1991

The Media as a System of
Thought Control

The Propaganda System

Noam Chomsky

October 24, 1986

DB: You've talked extensively about the politics of language and semantics, and you've said, "We have to peel away veil after veil of distortion to see the truth." My question is, in the age of Orwell, and given the U.S. educational system, what intellectual tools is that system providing to students to decode, decipher and translate those Orwellian terms?

Let me first comment that, although we always, I too, call this the age of Orwell, the fact is that Orwell was a latecomer on the scene. The American public relations industry, which is a very sophisticated industry, already in the early 1920s was developing these tools, writing about them, and so on. In fact, even earlier, during the First World War, American historians offered themselves to President Woodrow Wilson to carry out a task that they called "historical engineering," meaning designing the facts of history so that they would serve state policy. That's Orwell, long before Orwell was writing. Shortly after that, American journalists like Walter Lippmann, the famous American journalist, said in 1921 that the art of democracy requires what he called "manufacture of consent," what the public relations industry calls "engineering of consent," another Orwellism meaning "thought control." The idea was that in a state in which the government can't control the people by force it had better control what they think. So, well before Orwell this was understood; the techniques were designed and had been implemented extensively.

As to what the schools teach to defend people against this, the answer is simple: zero. In fact, the schools are quite on the opposite side: they are part of the disinformation apparatus. In fact, this is well understood, too. It's even well understood by liberal intellectuals, democratic theorists, and so on. For example, in the important study called *Crisis of Democracy,* another Orwellism meaning "beginnings of democracy," published by the Trilateral Commission, a group of international, essentially liberal elites, people of whom Carter was a kind of representative, the ones who staffed his administration, they refer to the schools as institutions responsible for "the indoctrination of the young." Of course, they're talking to one another there, that's not what you say in public. But that's the way they're understood. They are institutions for indoctrination, for imposing obedience, for blocking the possibility of independent thought, and they play an institutional role in a system of control and coercion. *Real* schools ought to provide people with techniques of self-defense, but that would mean teaching the truth about the world and about the society, and schools couldn't survive very long if they did that.

DB: C.P. Otero, who has edited a collection of your essays entitled *Radical Priorities,* has written in the preface of that book, "The totalitarian system of thought control is far less effective than the democratic one, since the official doctrine parroted by the intellectuals at the service of the state is readily identifiable as pure propaganda, and this helps free the mind." In contrast, he writes, "the democratic system seeks to determine and limit the entire spectrum of thought by leaving the fundamental assumptions unexpressed. They are presupposed but not asserted."

That's quite accurate; I've also written about that many times. Just think about it. Take, say, a country which is at the opposite end of the spectrum from us domestically, the Soviet Union. That's a country run by the bludgeon, essentially. It's a command state: the state controls, everybody basically follows orders. It's more complicated than that, but essentially that's the way it works. There, it's very easy to determine what propaganda is: what the state produces is propaganda. That's the kind of thing that Orwell described in *1984*—not a very good book, incidentally. One of the reasons it's so popular is because it's kind of trivial, and another reason is that it's talking about our enemies, so that makes it popular. If he was dealing with a serious problem, ourselves, then it wouldn't have been popular; in fact, it probably wouldn't have been published. In a country like that, where there's a kind of Ministry of Truth, propaganda is very easily identifiable. Everybody knows what it is, and you can choose to repeat it if you like, but basically it's not really trying to control your thought very much; it's giving you the party line. It's saying, "Here's the official doctrine; as long as you don't disobey you won't get in trouble. What you think is not of great importance to anyone. If you get out of line we'll do something to you because we have force."

Democratic societies can't really work like that, because the state can't control behavior by force. It can to some extent, but it's much more limited in its capacity to control by force. Therefore, it has to control what you think. And again, democratic theorists have understood this for 50 or 60 years and have been very articulate about it. If the voice of the people is heard, you'd better control what that voice says, meaning you have to control what they think. The method Otero mentions there is one of the major methods. One of the ways you control what people think is by creating the illusion that there's a debate going on, but making sure that that debate stays within very narrow margins. Namely, you have to make sure that both sides in the debate accept certain assumptions, and those assumptions turn out to be the propaganda system. As long as everyone accepts the propaganda system, then you can have a debate.

The Vietnam War is a classic example. In the major media, the *New York Times* or CBS or whatever—in fact, all across the spectrum except at the very far-out periphery which reaches almost no one—in the major media which reach the overwhelming majority of the population, there was a lively debate. It was between people called "doves" and people called "hawks." The people called hawks said, "If we keep at it we can win." The people called doves said, "Even if we keep at it we probably can't win, and besides, it would probably be too costly for us, and besides maybe we're killing too many people," something like that. Both sides, the doves and the hawks, agreed on something: we have a right to carry out aggression against South Vietnam. In fact, they didn't even admit that that was taking place. They called it the "defense" of South Vietnam, using "defense" for "aggression" in the standard Orwellian manner. We were in fact attacking South Vietnam, just as much as the Russians are attacking Afghanistan. Like them, we first established a government that invited us in, and until we found one we had to overturn government after government. Finally we got one that invited us in, after we'd been there for years, attacking the countryside and the population. That's aggression. Nobody thought that was wrong, or rather, anyone who thought that was wrong was not admitted to the discussion. If you're a dove, you're in favor of aggression, if you're a hawk you're in favor of aggression. The debate between the hawks and the doves, then, is purely tactical: "Can we get away with it? Is it too bloody or too costly?" All basically irrelevant. The real point is that aggression is wrong. When the Russians invaded Czechoslovakia, they got away with it, they didn't kill many people, but it was wrong because aggression is wrong. We all understand that. But we can't allow that understanding to be expressed when it relates to the violent actions of our state, obviously. If this were a totalitarian state, the Ministry of Truth would simply have said, "It's right for us to go into Vietnam," period. Don't argue with it. People would have known that that's the propaganda system and they could have thought what they wanted. They could have seen that we were attacking Vietnam just like we can see that the Russians are attacking Afghanistan. You couldn't permit that understanding of reality in this country; it's too dangerous. People are much more free, they can express themselves, they can do things. Therefore, it was necessary to try to control thought, to try to make it appear as if the only issue was a tactical one: can we get away with it? There's no issue of right or wrong. That worked partially, but not entirely. Among the educated part of the population it worked almost totally. There are good studies of this that show, with only the most marginal statistical error, that among the more educated parts of the population the government propaganda system was accepted unquestioningly. On the other hand, after a long period of popular spontaneous opposition, dissent and organization, the general population got out of control As recently as 1982, according to the latest polls I've seen, over 70 percent of the population still was saying that the war was, quoting the wording of the Gallup poll, "fundamentally wrong and immoral," not "a mistake." That is, the overwhelming majority of the population is neither hawks nor doves, but opposed to aggression. On the other hand, the educated part of the population, they're in line. For them, it's just the tactical question of hawk *vs.* dove. This is, incidentally, not untypical. Propaganda very often works better for the educated than it does for the uneducated. This is true on many issues. There are a lot of reasons for this, one being that the educated receive more of the propaganda because they read more. Another thing is that they are the agents of propaganda. After all, their job is that of commissars;

they're supposed to be the agents of the propaganda system so they believe it. It's very hard to say something unless you believe it. Other reasons are that, by and large, they are just part of the privileged elite so they share their interests and perceptions, whereas the general population is more marginalized. It, by and large, doesn't participate in the democratic system, which is an elite game overwhelmingly, and people learn from their own lives to be skeptical, and in fact most of them are. There's a lot of skepticism and dissent and so on. But this is a typical example. Here's a case which is an interesting one because, while the technique of thought control worked very effectively, in fact to virtually 100 percent effectiveness among the educated part of the population, after many years of atrocities and massacres and hundreds of thousands of people killed and so on, it began to erode among the general population. There's even a name for that: it's called the "Vietnam Syndrome," a grave disease: people understand too much. But it's very striking, very illuminating to see how well it worked among the educated. If you pick up a book on American history and look at the Vietnam War, there is no such event as the American attack against South Vietnam. It's as if in the Soviet Union, say, in the early part of the 21st century, nobody will have ever said there was a Russian invasion of Afghanistan. Everyone says it's a Russian defense of Afghanistan. That's not going to happen. In fact, people already talk about the Russian invasion of Afghanistan— maybe they defend it, maybe not— but they admit that it exists. But in the United States, where the indoctrination system is vastly more effective, the educated part of the population can't even see that it exists. We cannot see that there was an American invasion of South Vietnam, and it's out of history, down Orwell's memory hole.

DB: Who engineers this, who pulls this off, who are the mandarins, or to use Gramsci's term, the "experts in legitimation"? Who are these people?

The experts in legitimation, the ones who labor to make what people in power do legitimate, are mainly the privileged educated elites. The journalists, the academics, the teachers, the public relations specialists, this whole category of people have a kind of an institutional task, and that is to create the system of belief which will ensure the effective engineering of consent. And again, the more sophisticated of them say that. In the academic social sciences, for example, there's quite a tradition of explaining the necessity for the engineering of democratic consent. There are very few critics of this position. There are a few: there's a well-known social scientist named Robert Dahl who has criticized this, and he pointed out—as is obviously true—that if you have a political system in which you plug in the options from a privileged position, and that's democracy, it's indistinguishable from totalitarianism. It's very rare that people point that out. In the public relations industry, which is a major industry in the United States and has been for a long time, 60 years or more, this is very well understood: in fact, that's their purpose. That's one of the reasons this is such a heavily polled society, so that business can keep its finger on the popular pulse and recognize that, if attitudes have to be changed, we'd better work on it. That's what public relations is for, very conscious, very well understood. When you get to what these guys call the institutions responsible for "the indoctrination of the young," the schools and the universities, at that point it becomes somewhat more subtle. By and large, in the schools and universities people believe they're telling the truth. The way that works, with rare exceptions, is that you cannot make it through these institutions unless you've accepted the indoctrination. You're kind of weeded out along the way. Independent thinking is encouraged in the sciences but discouraged in these areas, and if people do it they're weeded out as radical or there's something wrong with them. It doesn't have to work 100 percent, in fact, it's even better for the system if there are a few exceptions here and there; it gives the illusion of debate or freedom. But overwhelmingly, it works. In the media, it's still more obvious. The media, after all, are corporations integrated into some of the major corporations in the country. The people who own and manage them belong to the same narrow elite of owners and managers who control the private economy and who control the state, so it's a very narrow nexus of corporate media and state managers and owners. They share the same perceptions, the same understanding, and so on. That's one major point. So, naturally, they're going to perceive issues, suppress, control and shape in the interest of the groups that they represent: ultimately the interests of private ownership of the economy—that's where it's really based. Furthermore, the media also have a market—advertisers, not the public. People have to buy newspapers, but the reason is that otherwise advertisers won't advertise there. The newspapers are designed to get the public to buy them so that they can raise their advertising rates. But the newspapers are essentially being sold to advertisers via the public, which is part of the medium for selling newspapers to advertisers. Since the corporation is selling it and its market is businesses, that's another respect in which the corporate system or the business system generally is going to be able to control the contents of the media. In other words, if by some unimaginable accident they began to get out of line, advertising would fall off, and that's a constraint. State power has the same effect. The media want to maintain their intimate relation to state power. They want to get leaks, they want to get invited to the press conferences. They want to rub shoulders with the Secretary of State, all that kind of business. To do that, you've got to play the game, and playing the game means telling their lies, serving as their disinformation apparatus. Quite apart from the fact that they're going to do it anyway out of their own interest and their own status in the society, there are these kinds of pressures that force them into it. It's a very narrow system of control, ultimately. Then comes the question of the individual journalist, you know, the young kid who decides to become an honest journalist. Well, you try. Pretty soon you are informed by your editor that you're a little off base, you're a little too emotional, you're too involved in the story, you've got to be more objective, there's a whole pile of code words for this, and what those code words mean is "Get in line, buddy, or you're out." Get in line means follow the party line. One thing that happens then is that people drop out. But those who decide to conform usually just begin to believe what they're saying. In order to progress you have to say certain things; what the copy editor wants, what the top editor is giving back to you. You can try saying it and not believing it, but that's not going to work, people just aren't that dishonest, you can't live with that, it's a very rare person who can do that. So you start saying it and pretty soon you're believing it because you're saying it, and pretty soon you're inside the system. Furthermore, there are plenty of rewards if you stay inside. For people who play the game by the rules in a rich society like this, there are ample rewards. You're well off, you're privileged, you're rich, you have prestige, you have a share of power if you want, if you like this kind of stuff you can go off and become the State Department spokesman on something or other, you're right near the center of at least privilege, sometimes power, in the richest, most powerful country in the world, and you can go far, as long as you're very obedient and subservient and disciplined. So there are many factors, and people who are more independent are just going to drop off or be kicked out. In this case there are very few exceptions.

Let me just give you one example. In March 1986, came the major vote on contra aid. For the three months prior to that, the administration was heating up the atmosphere to try to reverse the congressional restrictions on aid to the terrorist army that's attacking Nicaragua, what they internally call a "proxy army," a proxy terrorist army attacking Nicaragua, which is of course what it is.—

DB: Also called "freedom fighters."

—To the public they call them freedom fighters. If you look at the internal documents they're a proxy army engaged in terrorism, but that's internal, so I'll call them by the accurate internal terms: proxy terrorist army. So the question is: Could we reverse the congressional restrictions on this? That was the government's problem. The first three months of that year were very interesting in that respect: how were the media going to respond to the government campaign to try to reverse the congressional vote on contra aid. I was interested, so I took the two national newspapers, the *Washington Post* and the *New York Times,* and I went through all their opinion pieces, every column written by one of their own columnists, every authored submitted opinion piece and so on for January, February and March. There were 85. Of the 85, all were anti-Sandinista. On that issue, no discussion was even tolerable. So, 85 out of 85 followed the party line: Sandinistas are bad guys. Incidentally, it's interesting that there is one person of those 85 who has written elsewhere, in a more nuanced fashion, but not here. Perhaps he knows that he never could have gotten in unless he took that position. So on the major issue: Are we against the Sandinistas?: 100 percent control. Not a whisper of debate. Now comes the next point. There are two very striking facts about the Sandinista government as compared with our allies in Central America: Honduras, Guatemala, El Salvador. These facts are undeniable,

whatever you think about them. One is that the
Sandinistas, among these Central American countries,
are unique in that the government doesn't slaughter its
population. That's just not open to discussion. That's a
fact. Second, it's the only one of those countries in which
the government has tried to direct services to the poor,
has in fact diverted resources to social reform. Again,
that's not under discussion. You can read that in the
Inter-American Development Bank reports or anywhere
you like. So these are two rather striking facts that differ-
entiate Nicaragua from Guatemala, El Salvador and in
fact even Honduras, where about half the population is
starving to death. Those three countries, especially Guatemala and El Salvador, are among the world's worst
terrorist states. In the 1980s, they have slaughtered
maybe over 100,000 of their own citizens with ample U.S.
support and great enthusiasm. They are simply violent,
terrorist states. They don't do anything for their population except kill them. Honduras is more like a government
where the rich rob the poor, that's the government. They
do some killing, but not on the scale of their major allies,
but maybe half the population is starving. In contrast, the
Sandinista government, whatever you think about them,
has not slaughtered the population and has diverted resources to them. That's a big difference. So the next thing
I looked at was: How often were those two facts mentioned
in these 85 editorials? The fact that the Sandinistas are
radically different from our allies in that they don't
slaughter their population was not mentioned once. No
reference to that fact. The fact that they have carried out
social services for the poor was referred to in two phrases
in 85 columns, both sort of buried. One was an oblique
reference which said that because of the contra war they
can't do it any more. It didn't say what they were doing.
The other was a passionate attack against the Sandinistas
as totalitarian monsters and so forth and so on, which said
that well, of course, they did divert resources to the poor.

So, two phrases in 85 columns on that crucial issue, zero phrases in 85 columns on the not-insignificant fact that, as distinct from our allies, they haven't slaughtered their population, they haven't killed 100,000 people. Again, that's really remarkable discipline.

After that, I went through all the editorials in the *New York Times* from 1980 to the present—just editorials—on El Salvador and Nicaragua, and it's essentially the same story. For example, in Nicaragua on October 15, 1985, the government instituted a state of siege. This is a country under attack by the regional superpower, and they did what we did in the Second World War in Hawaii: instituted a state of siege. Not too surprising. There was a huge uproar: editorials, denunciations, it shows that they're totalitarian Stalinist monsters, and so on. Two days after that, on October 17, El Salvador *renewed* its state of siege. This is a state of siege that had been instituted in March 1980 and has been renewed monthly since, and it's far more harsh than the Nicaraguan state of siege. It blocks freedom of expression, freedom of movement, virtually all civil rights; it's the framework for mass slaughter within which the army we organized has carried out massive torture, slaughter, and is still doing it, in fact.

All you have to do is look at the latest Amnesty International report. So here, within two days, Nicaragua instituted a state of siege, and El Salvador renewed its state of siege under which they had carried out a major mass slaughter and torture campaign. The Nicaragua state of siege was a great atrocity; the El Salvador state of siege, which was far harsher in its measures and its application, literally was not mentioned. Furthermore, it has never been mentioned. There is not one word in about 180 editorials which mentions it, because that's our guys, so we can't talk about it, they're a budding democracy so they can't be having a state of siege. In fact, the editorial comment and the news reporting on El Salvador is that this is somehow a moderate centrist government which is under attack by terrorists of the left and terrorists of the right, which is complete nonsense. Every human rights investigation, the church in El Salvador, even the government itself in its own secret documents, concedes that the terrorism is by the centrist government; they are the terrorists. The death squads are simply the security squads. Duarte is simply a front for terrorists, as he knows. But you can't say that publicly because it gives the wrong image. You can go on and on, but these are very dramatic examples of the utter servility of the media right at the top. They will not even permit opinion pieces, not only editorials, even opinion pieces won't be permitted which stray from the party line, because it's just too dangerous. Similarly, throughout the whole Vietnam War there was never an opinion piece in the *New York Times* or any other newspaper that I know of that said that the United States was wrong to attack South Vietnam. Here's a research project for someone: if you can find one word in any opinion piece in any American newspaper or in the media, I'd be very surprised. I haven't read everything, of course, but I've been following it pretty closely for years, and I've never seen it.

DB: Is the control of capital the source, the bedrock of power in the American state?

Certainly, there's no doubt of it. The first Chief Justice of the Supreme Court and the President of the Constitutional Convention, John Jay, expressed it very accurately: he said, "The people who own the country ought to govern it." And that's the way it works. There are all sorts of mechanisms. For one thing, they have the resources to participate in politics. They can get information, they can put pressure, they can lobby, they can build platforms, they, in fact, are the real market for the political parties, they allow the parties to survive. They staff the executive, by and large, they staff Congress even.

Furthermore, if any government ever got out of line, even in the slightest way, they could stop it simply by cutting back investment, by capital flight, and so on. Here this isn't a problem, because the corporations so totally own the government that it never gets out of line. But in other countries, especially third world countries, that problem sometimes arises, and then very quickly, if the government tries to carry out social reform, it's stopped. Why? Just a little bit of capital flight is enough to do it, and it means the country grinds to a halt. So an effective control over the basic decisions in the society is in private hands, narrowly concentrated, that's going to control the state.

Like a Small Trout on a Heavy Line

Ben Bagdikian

March 14, 1991

DB: What are the trends that you have traced in the concentration of media in the United States, starting with the first edition of *The Media Monopoly* in 1983 and the latest edition, 1990?

There had always been change in the United States since newspapers got to be an industry in the late nineteenth century, but there were just a few of them. The vast majority of newspapers were owned by either individual families or groups of them or local people. Then, beginning about twenty five or thirty years ago, it began to be seen by Wall Street that in fact the daily newspaper industry is fabulously profitable. It's one of the most profitable industries in the country, right up there with pharmaceuticals and tobacco. For that and a number of reasons, larger corporations became interested in newspapers as properties, or major papers began buying other papers, with a very permissive government policy that permitted all kinds of tax breaks for buying other papers and also narcotizing the anti-trust laws. This seemed to grow so rapidly during the 1970s and 1980s that I did the book that you mentioned, which came out initially in 1983. I looked at all the major media at that time: daily newspapers, of which there are now about 1,600, magazines, and there are over 11,000 different ones, radio, television, about 10,000 stations, books, with over 2,500 publishers, and movies. I used a relatively conservative measure. I took each of these individually, the newspaper business, for example, and saw which companies had half or more of the business. I did that progressively through all of these other media. When you put them all together there were fifty corporations that had half or more of all the business in daily newspapers, magazines, radio, television, books and movies. This continued with great speed during the 1980s. There were many consolidations, conglomerations and takeovers, and by the time I did the third edition, which came out in 1990, those fifty corporations had shrunk to twenty six, and I believe it's smaller than that now. The trend, I think, continues in practically all the media.

DB: What's driving that concentration? Is it solely profit motive?

Primarily it's profit motive, but only primarily. There is an associated motive. I happened to get a transcript of a session between big investors and someone who was in the newspaper selling business, a broker. He told these investors that there are two reasons to buy newspapers. One is profit. The other is influence. It's obvious what the influence is. It's to have a major effect on what the public knows in information, ideas, values, and what it doesn't know. But there is another influence which I think has not received enough attention. It's an influence on government behind the scenes, that is to say, in lobbying, in pressuring for favorable legislation and regulation, taxes and so forth. All large corporations have disproportionate influence on government policy in the sense that they have large lobbies and expensive law firms in Washington, which the ordinary citizen does not have. But no one has as much attention given to it when it asks the government for favors as the media corporations have. It takes no angel from heaven to tell a politician that when the owner of eighty or a hundred newspapers or who controls getting to maybe a hundred million Americans on broadcasting or a major book house, that that politician's image before the public is controlled by this person. So that person gets a very respectable hearing. That helps explain why, for example, the policies of the Federal Communications Commission have permitted even more concentration than in the past, in which newspapers and broadcasters, since newspapers are major owners of broadcasting and cable, have deregulated cable, which is now an unregulated monopoly in 98 percent of cases, and why, for example, the tax benefits have been better for larger corporations than for small ones, and the anti-trust laws have not been observed hardly at all anyway, but certainly not as far as the media are concerned.

It makes a difference in not only the laws and regulations as far as fairness for the whole population is concerned, but it makes things more difficult for smaller operators in the media. The whole underlying principle of the First Amendment is that there should be as many conflicting and competing voices, not just economically, but in ideas and perspectives and information, as possible and that it has been one of the central parts of the American rhetoric that we are against centralized government control of information, as well we ought to be. Centralized control of information by government means censorship. We ought to be very concerned with centralized control when it's private as well as governmental. At the very least, if it's governmental people can vote out the censor. When it's private, they can't.

DB: If the American newspaper industry is, as you say, "fabulously profitable" and if that is so, why do 98 percent of American cities that have newspapers have only one?

The daily newspaper business, with the exception of a handful of cities, is a local monopoly. The basic reason for that is that over the decades newspapers have come to depend more and more on mass advertising. For the mass advertiser, it is much more efficient to advertise in one large newspaper, for a whole series of stores that may cover a whole market or a whole region, than it is for half a dozen papers to have to carry ads. So as a paper becomes larger and more powerful, the advertiser shifts more and more to that number one paper. That makes good business sense in one way, because you want to get your ads into as many households as efficiently as possible. Ads—and money—are shifted to the number one paper, away from the number two, three and four papers. So over the decades those other papers disappeared. We have in 98 percent of American cities that have any daily paper a monopoly management. In half of those there isn't even combined business partners, as there is in one percent.

DB: The role of advertising is clearly critical. Also there is the notion of the "right reader" or the "right consumer" of news. In your book your cite an incident dealing with the *New Yorker* magazine in 1967 when it turned against the Vietnam War and suffered an acute drop in advertising income.

It is true in all advertising supported media, with very few exceptions, that they want the good consumers because that's what the advertisers want. Newspapers and any medium that controls where it is sold have gone out of their way to push circulation, as do magazines, in the affluent postal zones, the affluent suburbs and neighborhoods and away from the non-affluent. But they do it in another way. Their editors are told where the affluent neighborhoods are and are told to select the news of interest to those people. Gradually those issues and that information that affect the non-affluent begin to diminish in the news. I think that's contributed to the polarization of our society which we're seeing now between those who are getting richer and richer and those who are getting poorer and poorer. Governmental policies have been basically the cause of that, but the mass media, which have concentrated on the more affluent for advertising purposes, have been less concerned with what now represents, I think, over half the population because the ideal target for mass advertising is an affluent person or household with people in it between the ages of 18 and 49. There are a lot of people in our society who are over 49. There are a lot of people below the median income, and they aren't terribly important to those media that have control of where they go. In broadcasting, broadcasting can't control who receives them. It goes out and poor families get it as much as rich families. As a matter of fact, the data are quite clear that the more affluent and educated the less they watch television. So you would think the best customers would be the non-affluent. They are not ignored in the numbers, because broadcasters like to boast about their ratings. Ratings mean a lot of money. One percent of a rating for a prime-time show on a network is worth between $30 and $60 million of revenue a year, which is why people are fired, programs are dropped with only one or even a fraction of one percent change in the ratings. But they are still interested in selling themselves as the medium for the good consumer.

If you look at what they produce to advertising agencies and to their major advertisers, it isn't just saying, we have 20 percent or 30 percent of the audience. They have stacks of computerized data which say, yes, but our audience has a very large proportion of people, larger than our competitors, who buy wine by the case and have two expensive cars and take expensive vacations and fly first class on airlines. They are pushing the same thing. That's one thing that is happening. The news and needs about the non-affluent have been gradually strained out of our media until they begin to disappear. When they disappear in the mass media they tend to disappear in politics, and something else happens which is dangerous and tragic. That means that we are getting to be a society that no longer has the old-fashioned democratic institutions of the same school where everybody lived and the neighborhoods where there were poor, middle and affluent people within walking distance of each other and who took mass transit downtown and rode the same trolley, same bus, etc. What we have are separated neighborhoods, physically, more and more separated schools, and now we're getting separated media, so that these populations live in increasing ignorance of each other. That's dangerous, because there is lack of empathy, understanding and concern on both sides.

DB: You've commented that there was a tremendous dropoff in government support for public housing during the Reagan administration and the consequent growth in homelessness and that the media were very slow, if at all, to pick up on that.

The media have had, in most places, that is, newspapers and occasionally in broadcasting, stories about the homeless, and they do have stories about poor people.

DB: But not making that political connection.

Right. I think that's the point. What they do is produce sometimes a story that is very tragic about the poor widow and maybe about a homeless person whose family had to live in their car and the car breaks down and the next thing you know they're in the street. But it leaves the public with the idea that this is an act of God. But the homeless were not with us ten years ago. We did not have a large, growing beggar class ten years ago, and there are real reasons for that. There are some very simple, documentable reasons. The news media like to say, we've got to have solid evidence. There are a number of things that have produced the homeless.

Just let me give one example. During the 1970s, the
government subsidized 200,000 medium and low income
housing units per year. During the 1980s, 17,000. What
does that mean? That means that the moderate income
housing that used to be occupied by the family with two
members who worked at minimum wage jobs. Suddenly,
with the shortage of housing, middle income people were
competing for that house. We know that they did compete.
Gradually it's cascaded downwards so that the working
class, lower middle income families can no longer afford
to buy a house in most cases and they now occupy the
places that poorer working class people occupied. We don't
see that in the newspapers. The reasons for it, the political, social reasons, tend not to be given. Why? Because if
we knew that there would be a growing understanding by
the public and a demand for change in social policy.
Instead of being irritated and angry at the homeless, we
would see that there's something that can be done besides
giving them a dollar or a quarter or helping out individual
cases or even resenting the fact that they are a kind of
rebuke to us. I think the reasons are there, but they're not
given because that's another thing that happens when the
media have decided, the professionals of the media have
accepted, in a kind of subtle, socializing way, that there
are certain areas that are not really news.

The American journalist has been so accused by
conservatives for the last twenty years of being radical,
being hateful of the establishment, that the individual
journalist is inclined to bend over backwards to show that
he's fair to conservatives. We see what happened in the
Reagan years, the treatment by Washington correspondents. But I think if it were an opposite political
reaction, that is to say, if journalists were trying to show
that they were fair to liberals or to people supportive of
public sector spending, they would not be permitted to
lean over backwards, because while there is a high degree
of professionalism in technique among American journal-

ists, there is a leash of a sort. There is a kind of centrist-to-right ideology or point of view which is acceptable but there is not an equal acceptability for an equal time on the other side of the spectrum. That is not just accidental, because editors do assigning. Executive producers decide what will get on the networks and what will not. Executives decide what documentaries will be made and which will not be made. It isn't that the newspaper has a bare space where a story was not done or that the broadcast, heaven forgive, would have a moment of silence. Something fills that up. But that something does not pass usually over the line into something that would seriously question the status quo.

   DB: So there's not so much censorship from above as self censorship?

   There's self censorship that comes in this way, which as someone who has been a reporter and editor most of his adult life understands. I've probably been influenced myself. You don't write stories that you know are not going to appear in the paper. You don't work hard on something that's not going to get on the air. This doesn't mean that you do nothing, or that you do anything dull. You may do something very interesting. But if in the average place you come in and say, "I think that there are some very clear economic and social reasons why we see the homeless that explain why it's happened over the last ten years," I think most editors and executives in broadcasting would say, "Nobody's interested in that," or "Maybe another time, not now," or "There really isn't enough documentation," a professionally acceptable reason. Some reporters fight for that and get it in. Some editors and producers are somewhat more open than others. But on the whole, there are things that are not put in for what seem to be professional reasons: "Nobody's interested," "It's a downer," "Everything must be up and cheery," "People will tune off."

Therefore you don't put it in. So everything is hunky-dory. Those kinds of stories get in easily, that what's going on is fine. If there's a tragedy it's an act of God or there's no explanation, and the result is that there is hopelessness and frustration in the body politic.

The result is that increasingly people don't even bother to vote because politicians watch television. They read the newspapers. If the television or newspapers don't say, something has to be done about X, they shut up about X. There is a growing part of our population that does not hear in political campaigns things that affect their lives in a direct way, and they've tuned out. I think part of that is the tuning out of those issues by the media themselves.

DB: So in some ways you're going along with the current political line in that the media can set and can create an agenda if they decide to focus on AIDS or housing or these other issues, then it will become part of the public agenda?

I don't think there's any question that the news media, and even the entertainment media, are major influences on the national agenda. We know that in a locality, for example, if the local newspaper campaigns on something, chances are something will happen. I think that's true on a national basis. But there is no question that they help set the public agenda. They sometimes deny that, saying, we just reflect public opinion. There's a lot of public opinion that does not show up in their paper because they're outside this desirable advertising audience and because it might upset the political and economic status quo that is now so favorable to large corporations, some of whom are now major owners in the media.

DB: In 1973 Noam Chomsky and Edward Herman wrote a book called *Counterrevolutionary Violence*. It had a rather curious and strange journey. In fact, the book was never published. What happened?

That was a case in which an editor who had been putting out readers, background books for political science and public affairs courses in colleges, had been quite successful in a publishing house. In the process of conglomeration and buying up the media, Warner Publications picked up this academic publisher. Academic publishing can be very profitable. If you get a text adopted by the University of Texas, you sell thousands and thousands of copies. If you get your book accepted as background reading or a text in a state, you've got wholesale sales right away. It's a good business when it's going. So they bought this house. This was coming out of the 1950s, 1960s, and 1970s, in which American Cold War policies were very influential in what we accepted and didn't accept among other nations. One of them was that book, the theme of which was that the American government supported many regimes which were themselves violent and brutal and dictatorial, but they were anti-left, so they were acceptable and got economic and military aid. It was accepted by the same publishing house which did books and pamphlets across the whole spectrum. There were things that were on the other side of that fence. But it got to the head of Warner Books and William Sarnoff saw it with shock and horror. He was a great admirer of Richard Nixon. He ordered the books shredded before they could hit the academic conventions and the sales. They were shredded.

DB: You've written in an article in *The Nation* called "Lords of the Global Village" that the global media oligopoly is not visible to the eye of the consumer. Why not?

The consumer generally does not know who owns his or her media. It has a label, a logo, we all know the

network logos when we see it and hear it. We all know the
newspaper has a title and sometimes newspapers will
have names of editors and business managers and officials. But it isn't obvious that in, let's say, a town in
Kansas a paper's owned by a corporation and a hundred
miles away there's another paper that's owned by the
same corporation and fifty miles from there another paper
is owned by the same corporation, and so forth. Or that
with TV stations in the biggest markets they are owned
by the networks, not just affiliates, it's not something
that's broadcast all the time. It's a business item. There's
very little way that the consumer can get a feeling that
there is this concentration of ownership. Many of these
media are local and people listen to their local stations.
Who owns the station is a thousand miles away and is of
no concern to them. It is of great concern in terms of
national influence, but for the individual viewer or reader
that isn't something that looms big.

DB: One of the notions that has permeated popular
culture in terms of the Vietnam War is how the media
were culpable in the loss of Vietnam.

Yes, and I'm afraid we're going to be stuck with that
now with the results of the Middle East war. Of course it's
nonsense. The Vietnam War had gone on for fifteen years
before a handful of reporters began reporting from the
field what the military officers in the field themselves
wanted to get out, which was they're lying about what
we're doing. These body counts are fake. The officers were
disgusted. American involvement in Vietnam began in
1954. The *Pentagon Papers* appeared in the early 1970s.
That's when the documentation of the lying appeared. It
had been preceded by a few stories, a few correspondents
that showed that number one, we were not winning the
war. We announced every year that we had practically
won the war. The body counts and the tonnage had not

made much difference. If anything, we were losing the war. It was not because of the media. The media had been very supportive. It's astonishing if you look at the record, the *New York Times,* the *Washington Post* editorially supported the war right up until the very end, as with practically every paper, practically every network.

One of the things that *did* happen where the media had an influence, unwittingly, was that some of the footage, including footage that was released by the Army and given to the networks, showed on TV screens in American homes that war is ugly. We have to remember that we have not had a war in our territory since the Civil War. That memory is long gone. No one is alive now who knew what it was like to have blood shed in your back yard or front yard and your house smashed. It's been a distant thing. What happens is that soldiers come back and there are victory parades and flags flying and the story that we got always was how our glorious troops were winning. That's true of every country.

The media have interesting studies, that show historically the news people of each country became boosters for their own country and screened out the things that were unpleasant and boosted the things that were pleasant. Suddenly, we had television in the living room with footage that the military had approved of or made accessible for camera people that showed that there were children, women and civilians who were being hurt by the war. It became increasingly clear that not only were we losing the war, we certainly weren't winning the war. We had 55,000 casualties. We happened to kill two million Indochinese, but the American casualties themselves were a shock to people. There was a realization that the good guys and the bad guys, regardless of how you define them, fight the same kind of war, which is to kill or be killed. That anything that gets in the way must be smashed. That's the way you fight a war. It's in the nature of war. We could always sugar coat that before because it was so distant. Even if it appeared in print it wasn't vivid. On television you could see the civilian huts burning, you could see the women and children crying and see them injured and hurt. That was one of the things that caused the change.

DB: Daniel Schorr of National Public Radio told me that he had been in conversation with some senior military officers, all of whom had served in Indochina and had a deep resentment toward the media and were quite frank about their intention to control the news in future wars. Could you reflect on that in terms of what has happened in Grenada, Panama and now in Iraq?

I think there's no question that that's true. The skill, not just in the military, but in the White House, in controlling and influencing the media to produce what they wish to have produced has become very great, when it isn't blunt. In a war it's very blunt: You shall not go to this place and you shall not run anything that we don't approve of. But even before that there was increasing skill which the media themselves, the news professionals, have not kept up with in terms of being able to deal with that. They are given their photo opportunities which then become the picture on television and on the front page. They're given their sound bite, which is the only message that comes out that day. There are other techniques to eliminate as much dissent as possible. The military did that in Grenada. They did it in Panama and got away with it. One reason they got away with it is the media's fault themselves. They were not permitted to see at the time of the invasion of Panama, for example, that there were serious blunders, widespread civilian damage and deaths, and that it left the country a mess. That was at the time the actual fighting was going on. They were very tightly secluded and kept away from that. After the fighting ended, they were free to go down and report what really happened, and for the most part the main media did not do that. I think that emboldened the military to believe that if you control it at the time, by the time the interest shifts to something else, it's a dead issue in the media. They aren't going to go back and tell what really happened. So in a sense the media asked for it. And the government succeeded. The media have not gone back. They had plenty of reason in other ways to know that.

For most of the Reagan administration, Central America was the center of American foreign policy. The major media took most of their news from the American Embassy, the White House, the National Security Council and the Department of Defense. With very few exceptions they did not have resident correspondents who got to know the country, who spent time and looked at the whole picture with comprehensiveness and continuity. So they got away for a long time with the idea that the *contras* were all freedom fighters and they were not in the drug trade and they didn't do nasty things to civilians but that the Sandinistas did. For a long time the Salvadoran army was the defender of freedom in El Salvador. For a long time we suppressed information that came out of Costa Rica that said that the *contras* were in fact drug dealing, including Colonel North, or was working with people he knew were. They got away with it. I think that that's emboldened the government to feel that not only can they control the information but that the media will do very little to go back and tell the whole story in an effective way. I think that that's happened in the Middle East. Because the Middle East was such an overwhelming American military victory, for which the full force of the American military force was designed to fight a country like the Soviet Union, the public seems to have accepted the idea that one important element was to censor the press and the news media. I think we're going to suffer from that for a long time.

DB: I believe you've written that the great strength of American reporting and journalism is its presentation of facts, its attention to and gathering of facts. I wondering how you could say that, within the context of the Iraq war. On August 2 all of a sudden war erupts for no plausible reason. Saddam Hussein invades Kuwait. A long history of U.S. support for Saddam Hussein is not put into any kind of historical context. The American people are presented with this "naked aggression."

There are facts and there are facts. All the things that you have said are true. The agency in the United States which is supposed to control the export of militarily useful things permitted $1.5 billion worth of licenses for militarily useful things to Saddam Hussein. That's a fact. He invaded Kuwait. That also is a fact. Those two facts are seldom reported in any kind of relationship to each other. So the American journalist is very skilled, in fact superior to many foreign journalists, in being careful about facts, being careful of getting those things accurately.

DB: My point is that they don't get the facts. For example, the Savings and Loan scandal, or the Iran/*Contra* affair.

They were very careful in reporting the facts that, for example, when the Reagan administration officials said deregulation will take government off the backs of business and everybody will be better off. They really did say that, and the reporters really did report that very accurately. What they didn't report was what other people with great credentials were saying: Wait a minute. We went through this in the 1920s. We're going to suffer if that happens because of A, B, C, and D. Some very credentialed people were saying that. That was not reported.

So what I'm saying is, yes, the factual accuracy of quoting the president probably is as high as anyone could ask. But the attempt to get facts which are relevant from people who are in a position to speak with knowledge is not pursued when it is in direct conflict with voices of authority. Or it is pursued so spasmodically and with such obscurity that it has very little impact. Just before the shooting started in the Gulf War, we saw for the first time in our major media for about two or three days very serious arguments on why we should not go into a shooting war, arguing that we should use the sanctions. We saw it because these were former Chairs of the Joint Chiefs of Staff. They were impeccable military people, powerful people at one time. It was hard to ignore them. They were testifying before a powerful Senate committee. That got in. As soon as the shooting began, that part of it ended. Then it became a dramatic physical story which then was controlled because it was a war zone and the military people control what was shown. What was shown was a kind of giant Nintendo game in which nobody got hurt.

DB: I know of constant reports about the marvelous accuracy and wonder of American weapons, but very little about what was at the other end of those bombs.

Also, military people are now saying that the accuracy is somewhat overrated, that the smart bombs were at best 60 percent smart. They're technologically extremely ingenious, but they get confused and hit schoolhouses instead of military bunkers, and some of them aren't smart at all, they're just heavy, brutal bombs. That's the way you fight a war. But you should not blink at it. The problem is this: we depicted it as though this is done remotely by fancy machines and we suffered almost no casualties when you come to think of a half million force; that it is a painless process. It's like violence on television. Everybody gets up and goes home. It makes you forget what happens if you decide to go to war.

A country may decide to go to war, I personally thought we were correct to enter World War II, although I was a pacifist before that. But it must know it's going to be ugly, violent and things will disturb everybody in it. Every fighting soldier on both sides is scarred forever by it plus all the terrible maiming and killing of people who are not soldiers. It's one thing to do that knowingly.

But if you can sell a war as a painless Nintendo game, people will be much more ready to buy it. The military fear public resistance; that's what leaders fear when they decide that they want to settle things in a military way. They want unity at home so they control that kind of information, and they don't want to remind people that a lot of people are going to get hurt, and these are going to be a lot of innocent people, too.

DB: What about the politics of sources? It seems that if you're talking about praising American journalists for being so precise with their facts, if they're constantly going to the Pentagon and Defense Department sources, etc., they're not really embracing diverse points of view.

No. Diversity of viewpoints is not considered legitimate unless that diversity goes only so far as the voices of authority, the people with high titles. That's overstating; it's even more restrictive than that.

During the 1980s, most of what we read about mergers, acquisitions, takeovers, junk bonds were the exciting fights on Wall Street: who won, who lost, which one of the raiders won, which one of the raiders lost, what this company was going to be worth before and after. Information about strictly the exchange of money and power within this powerful elite. There were people who were economists in good standing who were not on the Council of Economic Advisors, not in the Treasury Department, not White House officials, who were saying, "We're headed for trouble. You deregulate your savings and loan and we're going to be in real trouble. You're going to lose mortgages for middle-class people and they're going to start speculating on the junk bond market." People who were saying that who were good economists, who had plenty of credentials, but they were not heard, not quoted. If they were it was on the 27th paragraph on page 23 with most of the story dominated by the bankers who were making money on this and the raiders who were in this game of creating funny paper.

But papers knew about it. A few papers did things. Nobody picked it up, and papers don't like to be out on a limb, so they dropped it. So voices that are contrary to high authority have trouble getting in the news. Frequently those are the voices that most need to be heard, the voices that have a basis for speaking with some knowledge. There were plenty of those, but they were not asked. If they were it was only as an afterthought at the very end.

DB: Another trend which I'd like to know your opinion on is the celebrity status of the anchors and reporters themselves and the enormous salaries that they command. Is that something that concerns you?

Yes. I think the worst thing that can happen to a journalist professionally is to become a celebrity. Celebrity for television people is a commercial artifact. It is useful. The more someone is known as a personality, the easier it is to promote this person as a combination entertainment and news commodity. So they fly anchors off to the scene in their trenchcoats and their open throat shirts in a windblown scene and they've been there maybe six hours. They may have very little depth in what they're reporting, but they're a celebrity, a personality, and it's very successful on television. People have a tendency to

be sympathetic with a known personality. It's a good
commercial commodity. It's not good news.

For print people, where the notoriety tends to depend
on how often they appear on television, it's less so. Still,
to a lesser degree it's true, too. What you do to maintain
your status as celebrity is antithetical to what you do in
being a journalist who is observing. As a celebrity you're
concerned with yourself as part of the scene. As a journalist you're supposed to be concerned with the scene, minus
you.

DB: To get back to the Iraq war: a rather bizarre
thing happened, at least from my perspective, in terms of
the reporting. Months before the war started we were
bombarded with accounts of the elite Republican Guard,
these battle hardened, terrific Iraqi troops. It was like a
Nazi war machine. Saddam Hussein was compared to
Hitler and Iraq was compared to Nazi Germany. You have
a smile on your face as I'm recounting these things to you.
The press just repeated all of these things without really
doing much investigation. When the Iraqi army completely collapsed, Thomas Friedman and others were
writing in the *New York Times* that the invincibility of the
Iraqi military was a myth.

I think the authorities got away with a number of
myths. First of all, some of the best authorities we have
on nuclear weaponry said that at best Hussein might have
one device at the end of the year that would not be
militarily useful, if he could do that. The chemical warfare, I think there's no question that he used it. One does
not have to regard Saddam Hussein as St. Francis of
Assisi to have to say what are the realistic facts, militarily,
economically and politically, about someone with whom
you're going to go to war. The Republican Guard may in
fact be a very powerful military army in Middle Eastern
terms. They are not a powerful army among the major

nations of the world. We beat them with a force that was designed to fight the second most powerful country in the world. So if you take Iraq, which is a very small country, compared to many other Middle Eastern countries highly developed industrially, I don't think there's any question about this, which is what made them vulnerable to sanctions if we'd been willing to try that.

But they were supposed to have the fourth strongest army. They may have been. But what does that mean? After you get number one and number two it drops off very quickly. Furthermore, I think it is probably true that even if the Republican Guard was everything that we said it was, if the front line troops—of whom we may have killed 100,000, conscripts, seventeen year olds, etc.—if they were well organized, the pounding they took I'm not sure any army could withstand. We had the most powerful weapons that have ever been used in warfare short of nuclear bombs with a tonnage that has never been equalled since Vietnam, which was more than all the bombs dropped in World War II, and we could operate in the air without opposition. I don't think the Soviet Army could have withstood that if they didn't have air defenses. Let us assume that it was a powerful army, but powerful in Middle East terms, not in world terms. I think that they were up against overwhelming force, cleverly used, but it is a mistake to think that it was a fight between equals.

The barbarities, as we will see, are something that Hussein has committed on some of his own people, and that is not unknown among our allies in this fight. Up until Saddam Hussein became our designated enemy, Mr. Assad of Syria was our designated enemy. Before that it was Iran. They became friends to us in this alliance. It's not a sentimental business. But the media ought to report the reality as closely as it can, rather than the exaggerated statements standing by themselves without also reporting known information that contrasts with that out of the White House. Hussein is a barbaric megalomaniac, but he's not Adolf Hitler. Iraq had a powerful military force in Middle Eastern terms, but it was not Nazi Germany, nor was it the Soviet Union. In that sense it was hitting a hornet with a bomb.

DB: Talk if you would about public broadcasting, specifically the two crown jewels, as it were, for television *MacNeil-Lehrer* and for radio National Public Radio. What are your views on those two programs?

I think they both serve an important, useful purpose, to be somewhat more thoughtful, less concerned with making sure that there is something new and different every thirty seconds. People are frequently permitted to say a paragraph. On the whole, I would say more useful than the average local news and the average network news.

Unfortunately, they are starved for funds. They increasingly depend on corporate sponsorship. The effect of corporate sponsorship on public television is very dramatic. It is not unreasonable for Coca-Cola or Pepsico or Mobil to say, "We'd rather not be the sponsors for a debate on abortion, because half the audience is going to hate what's said and they're going to hate our product. So let's not have anything controversial. Public affairs will be controversial. But we'll support *Live from Lincoln Center,* programs about furry animals in New Zealand, things that aren't going to make people angry." That's not the function of public television or radio. They are supposed to be a service which is not driven by money profit but which fills a need for information, insight, ideas and not necessarily commercial entertainment.

So it is superior to the commercial networks in that sense, if taken as a whole. But increasingly, as it is starved for funds, it depends on sponsorship that makes it like the commercial broadcasters. When you watch public television now, you use the mute button on your remote control almost as often as you do with the commercial networks. From a dignified placard which says: This program has been sponsored by X, you now get a regular commercial.

DB: What are your views on National Public Radio? Do you listen to it?

I think National Public Radio is an extremely useful service. It has an influential audience: people driving home who get from it a much more coherent and knowledgeable account of what's going on. I perceive a desire to make up for lack of money with some softness that's grown over the years and having to take corporate sponsorship from the Beef Council and others who would have some influence on the news. But compared to regular newscasts, it's incomparably better.

DB: There have been a plethora of books following *The Media Monopoly*. I'm thinking of Michael Parenti's *Inventing Reality,* Mark Hertsgaard, *On Bended Knee,* Chomsky and Herman, *Manufacturing Consent,* and most recently Norman Solomon and Martin Lee, *Unreliable Sources.* So now we have this whole body of literature talking about and criticizing the media. But so what? Have there been any changes?

I don't think there have been any changes of any consequence in the kinds of issues that we've been talking about. You have to remember that there's been a counterliterature that's much more widely distributed and put out by much more powerful people, that is convincing the owners of the media and many of the professionals that they really are unfair to conservatives and they must be much more careful about straying from the official line. While more and more journalists are personally bumping into some of the limitations that they weren't so conscious of before, it is an individual experience and not a collective one so it isn't so obvious to the profession as a whole.

There are journalism reviews, and some of them are very good at bringing up unfairness, bringing up limited sources that are in the end distorted because they are limited, but it has not changed practices overwhelmingly.

I do have to say something else. I think that the level of care in reporting in terms of getting different points of view is more evident on the local level than it is in Washington and New York. There you have intense competition, the headquarters of media organizations. The people who have power have learned how to feed these hungry, competitive fishes in Washington. You get a feeding frenzy to get the latest word from the top official. The top officials have learned how to play them like a small trout on a heavy line.

DB: What resources do you turn to for your news and information, and what can people do as consumers of news?

First of all, consumers of news are not a composite stereotype. They are different people who have different priorities in their news. That would determine a good deal of what they do. The major media do in fact carry a great deal of useful information. You have to look for it, read it carefully, but you can't do without it, to find out, if nothing else, what's in the minds of most of the country. You will find in most publications and most regular broadcasts things which will tell you that there is something there. In addition to that, if you're interested in education, in the economy, in social structure and what's happening to society, you have to do other things, too. You have to pay attention to the alternatives. Listen to public radio, public television, read magazines and books that pursue the subjects you're interested. You can't leave it just to the major news media.

Unfortunately, most people don't have time to become junior scholars in these things. But it is not an absence of information as much as the fact that it's not concentrated in the major channels that most people get most of their news from. You have to work a little harder than I wish you had to in reading around the edges of the major media, the edges meaning alternative publications, alternative broadcasting, listener supported broadcasting, reading books, getting magazines that pursue the subjects that you're interested in and have commentary and analysis. One of the things that's a problem with all information today is that we're flooded every day with a great deal. It tends to be undifferentiated bits of information.

What's needed is coherence, background, history, context, analysis, interpretation. There you're more apt to get it outside the major media which brings it all together and pursues whatever the consumer of news is most interested in in a much more understandable and clear way.

Propaganda and Class Structure

Some Working Definitions

Michael Parenti

August 16, 1988

DB: I want to talk to you about propaganda and its uses. "Propaganda" is defined as "the systematic propagation of a given doctrine," or "material disseminated by the proselytizers of a doctrine."

That definition itself might be a propagandist one. I suspect the lexicographers are Western ones and they believe that in the United States we don't have doctrines. We supposedly have an open approach to ideas. I would define propaganda as the mobilization of information and arguments with the intent to bring people to a particular viewpoint. In that sense there could be false and deceptive propaganda, and there could be propaganda that has a real educational value. You can after all inform people and mobilize them toward truth. In the United States the word "propaganda" is unrelievedly negative. In certain other countries, propaganda has a more neutral implication.

DB: There is definitely a pejorative connotation to it here. It conjures up images of Nuremberg rallies, the Nazi press, Goebbels, etc.

In socialist countries and in some other countries, too, in other languages, the word "propaganda" really means political publicity and political persuasion, which can be for good or bad.

DB: Is that generated by the state?

No, you can have a political group generating its propaganda. Peace propaganda, for instance, you hear people in revolutionary countries say we must make a large propaganda for peace. We must mobilize and develop a propaganda for this or that, in a positive way.

DB: What kind of propaganda exists in the United States today?

The first premise of propaganda in the United States today is that it doesn't exist, that there is no propaganda from the established media and from the government and that we have only "information." Propaganda is something that other people do. That's reflected in that definition of a doctrine. And nobody in the United States says they're selling or pushing a doctrine; they all say they're just reporting it like it is. That's the first premise: the denial that there is propaganda. The second quality of propaganda in the United States is that is operates all the time and its major dedication is to avoid any kind of confrontation regarding class struggle in the United States It denies any recognition that there is exploitation of labor, that the rich exploit the poor, that we exploit the third world, etc. We've now reached the point where you can talk about racism and sexism, but you cannot really talk about class power in America, and if you do, you are said to be engaging in propaganda.

DB: Why not? What mitigates against this kind of discussion?

You are labeled as being a Marxist, and a Marxist is presumed to be someone who has an axe to grind and wants to engage in class war. The propaganda in this country, the control of most symbols and debate is heavily class controlled. One of the goals of ruling class propaganda is to deny that it's class controlled. As Marx and Engels pointed out, they take their class interest and always try to represent it as the general interest.

DB: Could you be more specific about how the terms of debate are class controlled?

For instance, you cannot engage in any kind of debate about whether or not Nicaragua has a better society than it did before the revolution. In the political mainstream, the entire debate is whether or not we should be killing the Nicaraguans or in some other way pressuring and coercing and bullying them. The range of debate is about tactics: that is how to deal with Nicaragua. What's not mentioned is that the Nicaraguans have created a government, a movement and a state which is not dedicated to capitalism. It's not totally closed to private production, but its major dedication is to the social needs of its people. That becomes very dangerous. The ruling class cannot come out and say that openly; they cannot come out and say we've got to go die in Nicaragua to make it safe for capital penetration, investment, cheap labor markets, and extraction of resources.

What the ruling class does say is we must go into Nicaragua to restore the freedoms of the Nicaraguan people. What a joke. For 50 years under the Somocista butchery they had no democratic freedoms. What you would be restoring is fascism. They say, we've got to go in there for our own national security because the Russians are taking over Nicaragua. It is true that the Soviets are sending military aid to Nicaragua. What's never pointed out is that the Nicaraguans first asked for military aid from the United States and were denied that, and then they were invaded and attacked. So it's to the Soviets' credit that they gave them military aid. If they hadn't, the Nicaraguans would be in a more desperate situation than they are now. That, by the way, is another trait of propaganda: to not necessarily lie outright, but to leave out things, to suppress things. For instance, don't mention in all the reporting on Nicaragua that the U.S. has invaded Nicaragua 11 times in its history. Or if you mention it, don't explain why those invasions took place, or whose interests were being supported.

DB: You use the term "ruling class", and that triggers off all kinds of associations. What do you mean by that?

It's no secret. The Council on Foreign Relations was formed in 1922 by John D. Rockefeller, Sr., Nelson Aldridge and by J.P. Morgan. It's a council whose personnel are drawn from the corporate elite, with some college presidents, academics, news media people, and political leaders thrown in. The Council on Foreign Relations, the Committee on Economic Development, the Trilateral Commission are all organizations that have been formed, financed and staffed by these corporate elites. They provide the personnel who then serve in various administrations. The Council on Foreign Relations has placed its members as Secretary of the Treasury, Secretary of State or Secretary of Defense in every administration, whether its Republican or Democratic.

Jimmy Carter had 12 members of the Trilateral Commission in his cabinet, including himself and Walter Mondale. The Trilateral Commission was started by David Rockefeller. These elites have a capacity to place their members in the top decision-making positions unequalled by any other interest group in America. There's no labor union, no farmers' group, no teachers' group, there's no pro-abortion or anti-abortion group that could hope to place their leaders the way these people do. Their role is not to pursue the interests of any one particular corporation. Their role in these councils is to look at what are the common interests of all the various multinational corporations, what is the common interest, what is the common interest of the financial class.

DB: What are the mechanisms by which any discussion of ruling class interest or its nature are excised?

You can't talk about these kinds of things in the mainstream media because the media are owned by the very same people who staff these councils and staff our top decision-making positions. Capitalism is not only an economic system, it's an entire social order. Its function is not just to produce cars and refrigerators and make a profit for its owners. It also produces a whole communication universe, a symbolic field, a culture, a control over various social institutions like universities, museums and churches. Those of us who have a view which is anti-capitalist are frozen out, or we are consigned to small publications. You can say, well, you're consigned to small publications because you don't have that much to say or people don't care about what you're saying. It's not true. People would be interested in our message if they'd get a chance to hear it. And in any case, why not give them a chance to reject it? Why don't we get a chance to get on networks? Why don't we get the syndicated columns that appear in 300 newspapers? Why don't we get space in the mass-circulation magazines, in *Time* and *Newsweek?* Why don't we get commentaries on ABC, NBC, CBS? Why don't we get on Nightline?

DB: I'd like you to address the notion that the media are vigorous and independent or that they even have an adversarial relationship with state power. You have, for example, the January 1988 Bush/Rather confrontation on

CBS, which is cited as an example of a vigorous, skeptical and inquiring media.

There are differences among ruling class interests over tactics and emphasis. There are liberal capitalists and reactionary capitalists. There are those who want *détente* with the Soviets and those who want a mortal combat with the Soviets. Those differences among the ruling elites are often hard to contain and they break into the public view from time to time. It's then seen as a sign that there is diversity in our political life.

DB: You reject that notion?

No, I believe there is diversity within those limits. The debate between Rather and Bush is simply a debate between a fervently anti-communist liberal Democrat and a fervently anti-communist right-wing Republican over one or two issues. There are elements of diversity in the mainstream media. Things sometimes get in the media that are troublesome to their owners. Editors cannot exercise perfect censorship because they often don't even know the implications of a story. They might run a story and only later discover that it has unintended conse-quences and then they'll kill the story.

I'll give you an example. The story that General Noriega was involved in drugs. When that story came out it also came out that Colonel North was in constant communication with Noriega, that John Poindexter was in constant communication, that the National Security Council was chummy with Noriega. Then the question came up, surely we knew he was involved in drugs all these years. The guy was skimming hundreds of thou-sands of dollars. Suddenly they dropped that story. From then on they just talked about "strongman Noriega," "dic-tator Noriega," and how the United States was suddenly concerned about getting a democrat in there, a guy named

Devaille, who had the support of his family and the State
Department and maybe a portion of of the professional
class in Panama. They realized that the drug story was a
little too hot so they had to retreat from it and make it a
story of the U.S. government suddenly concerned about
restoring democracy in Panama.

There will be times when dissident perspectives can
come through because the ideological control isn't all that
efficient. Somebody might get something in, but only once.
Take, for example, the time Bill Moyers described imperialism in Guatemala. He talked about how a democrati-
cally elected government under Jacobo Arbenz in 1954
was overthrown by the CIA with the instigation of the
multinationals in a country where 2 percent of the population own 80 percent of the wealth and how today in
Guatemala there's no occupational safety controls, no
labor unions, no minimum wage, and much misery and
poverty. He was able to say that in his report on Central
America once. You never heard it again. So occasionally
little things like that will come in.

Also, there's a pressure on owners and publishers
that they sometimes have to grant their news organizations some modicum of independence. The news organizations themselves, to be able to exercise their class control
over the populace, also have to sell; they have to create a
product every day called "the news." It's a highly pro-
cessed manufactured product, and they have to sell it to
people. To sell it, it has to have some credibility. To be able
to exercise control you have to have credibility. To have
credibility you have to sometimes deal with the real world.
You can't say things like "We have nothing to do with
what's going on in Nicaragua," because everybody knows
we do. You can't say things like, "There's no pollution
problem." For the most part the media has to deal with
some of those issues, and when it does, it raises and
introduces troublesome questions. That then incurs the

irritation of the right wing or leaders like Ronald Reagan, who say, "why the hell do we have to print that stuff?"

If the right wing had its way, the media would be nothing but promo sheets for the ruling class: a lot of July 4th celebration-type stories and anti-communist horror stories and stories about the wonders of our economy and our system. By the way, a lot of newspapers in this country are little more than that. To the extent that some things do get through at times, this actually enhances the legitimacy of the media. I don't think the ruling classes appreciate what a terrific job the news media do in this country. You have people thinking our media are independent. When the right wing attacks them, they can portray themselves as independent. When the government complains about their stories, this puffs them up and gives them the illusion of independence.

D.B: How do the media achieve the appearance, as you call it, of objectivity?

By sometimes having to report troublesome news stories about troublesome things, sometimes having two or three different opinions on commentary shows, but the opinions will range from moderate Democrat to right-wing Republican. This will be taken as "diversity" and "objectivity."

DB: You call that a "false balancing."

Yes, false balancing because you're really excluding and censoring out the whole left part of the spectrum which involves a perspective shared by hundreds of millions of people throughout the world. That perspective is systematically suppressed, denied access to the media. Another false balancing is what *Nightline* does quite often: they say something like, "On Nicaragua you have the American view," and that will be a right-wing apologist like Elliott Abrams, and then the "opposing view" will be Ortega or some other Nicaraguan. So the Nicaraguan comes on. He has a foreign accent. He already has no legitimacy because he's a representative of his government. But the debate over Nicaragua's policy is an *American* debate, and it should be an American that goes on, who understands his American audience. On the arms debates, they have a guy from the Pentagon or State Department versus a Russian. The Russian would have an accent as thick as borscht, and sometimes would half understand the questions. He would give a response that was half understandable. That was the "opposing view." But there's a whole massive peace movement in America that has a position on the arms race, and it is not represented.

DB: In *Inventing Reality* you write, "The most effective propaganda is that which relies on framing rather than falsehood."

Framing is a way of bending the truth without breaking it. It's how much emphasis you give. If you put it in a headline on your front page you already are giving the reader the message that this is an important story. The way you use certain words, for instance, when Fidel Castro tried to get friendly relations with the U.S. a few years back, the *New York Times* ran a story saying, "What is Fidel Castro up to? What is he trying to do?" Already implying that there was some kind of machination involved here, rather than seeing this as a friendly overture. If you saw it as a friendly overture, that would raise all sorts of questions about U.S. policy toward Cuba. So the *Times* preferred to see him as manipulative, with something up his sleeve. Framing relies on the use of words, on placement, on a certain kind of vocabulary. If the Soviets walk out on negotiations, you can say that's evidence of their hostility. If they want to negotiate, then you quote government officials who say that this is just a propaganda ploy to throw us off our guard. You don't actually utter a lie, but you just mockingly make a point. I heard Dan Rather, for instance, point to an instance where the Soviets called for a reduction in conventional forces in Europe, some years ago, before the INF treaty. Rather, in a tone dripping with sarcasm, said that the U.S. did not consider this a serious offer and dismissed it. There was no lie told there. The Soviets did make this overture and the U.S. did reject it. But you were left with the impression that it was perfectly legitimate to reject the overture.

DB: You talk about the "graying of reality" in *Inventing Reality*. You cite a *New York Times* editorial, for example, on Salvador Allende in Chile in 1973. Would you discuss that?

There were stories, too, not just the editorials, which talked about how Allende "died" in the Moneda palace. He didn't die in the palace. He was murdered in the palace by Pinochet's fascist forces. It's not true that the media always go for the sensationalist thing. Quite often they downplay what are truly remarkable and sensational stories. They simply pass them over with a few muted words. Allende's death is a good example.

To take another instance of downplaying a sensational story, not long ago I saw a story in the *New York Times* which said way back in the inside pages, very deep into an article on Afghanistan, that the Afghan rebels were heavily involved in the opium trade and that as they took over more territory in Afghanistan we could expect that the outflow of opium would increase tremendously. This is just reported as a matter of fact, a tiny little paragraph. Imagine if that were the Nicaraguans who were involved in heroin and opium, imagine if that were the Salvadoran guerillas. It would have been splashed all over. It would be a major story treated every day with the

utmost urgency. We would hear about the narco-commu-
nists who are trying to subvert our society.

DB: There was, in fact, an attempt to link the
Sandinistas with drug-running.

There have been attempts to link the Sandinistas
with drug-running and there has been no evidence and
even our own Drug Enforcement Agency says there's no
evidence. The story didn't fly. Nobody in Latin America
believed it, and it just didn't go here. That's not framing
and not the graying of reality, that's just outright
disinformation. That's lying. But the graying of reality is
to take this remarkably sensational story about the
Mujahideen in Afghanistan, these murderers, feudal
tribesmen, Islamic fanatics, and drug pushers, and not
mention the fact that they are a major feed on the international drug trade. That's a sensational, remarkable
story which has been given very little play. What about
the sensational story of Three Mile Island? The media was
too busy reporting on Chernobyl all these months and
years to point out that today at Three Mile Island there
are farms where people are dying, sickened from cancer,
that farm animals are dying. I saw that on one little local
show, a little local documentary. It was horrifying. I
haven't seen anything in the major media. That's a sensational, mind-boggling story which the media have somehow been able to avoid.

Or let's take one last example: the air war in El
Salvador, which is financed, armed, supplied and supported by the United States military. The bombing of
liberated zones in El Salvador, the murdering of people,
dropping 500-pound bombs, 2000-pound bombs, destroying every living creature in these areas, and then sending
the army in to pour lye all over the soil and kill any
surviving livestock, to destroy and kill anything that
sustains life. This horrible war in El Salvador is not

reported. Project Censored voted it the most censored
story one year.

DB: This is an age of disinformation. Even the
disinformationists acknowledge that stories are indeed
fabricated. One could cite the Libyan hit squad hysteria
in the early 1980's, the plot to kill the Pope, KAL 007.
Where do these stories fit within the propaganda apparatus?

The disinformation stories wouldn't go anywhere if
it wasn't for the U.S. press obligingly portraying them. We
hear about the occasions when there are differences between the mainstream media and the government. What
we don't hear about are the other 95 percent of occasions
where the mainstream media faithfully propagate these
disinformation stories which are often planted by the CIA,
sometimes planted abroad in newspapers that they may
own or that are friendly to them and then through a
process of blowback the story is picked up and brought
here.

DB: Former CIA agent John Stockwell, in his book
In Search of Enemies, cites an example where he spread
a story that Cuban troops had raped and massacred
Angolans. This was reported faithfully in the U.S. press.

And in turns out it was a total fabrication. The
stories that the Vietnamese and Soviets have been using
chemical warfare in Afghanistan or Indochina are also
total fabrications. They haven't come up with a single
unexploded shell or shrapnel piece. The only "evidence" is
a few leaves with some fungus growth on them. The idea
that the Soviets would use this kind of chemical or
bacteriological stuff to wipe out a village is crazy. The
Soviet Army could take out a village in two minutes with
traditional artillery. It's been exposed as pure fabrication.
It was exposed here as a "mistake." Supposedly the U.S.

mistakenly saw bee feces and thought it was yellow rain. That's not true. The U.S. disinformation descriptions were of red, blue, green, all sorts of gases, they had fabricated elaborate descriptions, photos of people who were "poisoned."

DB: I'd like to talk to you about your experiences on radio talk shows. I know that you frequently travel around the country and you appear on these call-in shows. What has been your experience on those programs?

My experience is that when I'm on alternative radio, I get a chance to finish whole sentences and paragraphs. When I'm on mainstream radio and TV (I've done *Crossfire* twice, national TV shows), the format is to have me on with at least two opponents who then interrupt and cut in, scoff at what I have to say, quickly label me a Leninist or Marxist or whatever, and send certain cues out to their audience that "We've got a kook on our hands here who's got a personal axe to grind and who's discontent because we're not doing everything the way he wants it done." My view is I don't want any society to do everything the way I want it, I'd be worried about a society like that. But I'd like my perspective, which is not personal to me, but which is represented by millions of other people who organize and struggle, I'd like that perspective to be represented.

DB: How would you describe the phone calls that you get on these programs? Are they hostile, supportive, curious?

Sometimes they're hostile. If you have a right-wing host on a talk show, he already has developed a certain kind of Neanderthal following, so his listeners will be ready to pounce. But other times you may get surprisingly sympathetic callers, people who do not buy the official line and who point out that what I and others like me have to say is very important and has truth in it and deserves a fairer hearing than it is getting.

DB: What's your assessment of alternative media in the country today? There's a string of community radio stations, there are a few journals and newspapers here and there, do you see some movement in that area?

I think alternative media is our only hope, media like community radio stations like KGNU, and the *Guardian* and *Monthly Review, People's Daily World, In These Times, The Nation, The Progressive, Z* and other alternative publications. The trouble is that those with class power, those with lots of wealth, can reach tens of millions of people. Those of us with very little wealth can reach only a small audience market. Because of our viewpoint we can't attract much advertising. The advertisers are all part of the business class. So we have little publications with limited circulation teetering on the edge of insolvency. Most Americans have never heard of *The Nation,* which is by the way only a liberal magazine. That magazine has been publishing for 120 years, yet they haven't heard of it. There are more people in America today who have heard of and read *USA Today* than have read *The Nation,* and *USA Today* has been around for about seven or eight years. That's because Gannett can spend hundreds of millions of dollars to put their rag up on satellite and get instant distribution. Within a couple of years *USA Today* becomes the third-largest selling newspaper in the country. It's a bubble-gum newspaper, a newspaper of the television age with seven different colors, with stories rarely longer than 500 words. So it's not that demand creates supply, it's that supply creates demand. People could say, "Well, you on the left don't sell much because nobody's interested in your message." It's not true. The public doesn't even know we exist and they've never heard our message.

The reason they don't hear us is that we don't have
the hundreds of millions of dollars to reach those mass
markets. Ideas don't float around in space. Ideas are
mediated through material forces. All human activity has
a material base. That's the essence of Marxism. It's not
economic determinism, although Marxists don't rule out
economic determinism. The essence of historical materi-
alism is simply that all human activity has a material
base, and that material base is an ultimate determining
force in the development of human activity. Even the holy
guru who says material things mean nothing, spiritual
things mean everything, even he has to eat, and he is busy
getting money from his followers. Likewise with the dis-
semination of ideas. Given our limited material resources,
the alternative media reach limited audiences, but we
should keep at it.

DB: What's your analysis of "the left" today, and are
you comfortable with that term?

The left is a catch-all term to mean people who do
everything from opposing the business abuse of the envi-
ronment to opposing the intervention in Central America
to wanting the end of the Cold War, and support cuts in
military budgets. To people like myself who want the end
of multinational corporate capitalism itself and want
democratic socialism, I think the left is alive and well. I
have never believed we have been in a conservative mood,
I believe people voted for Ronald Reagan because the
economy was in such a mess and they were worried about
their buying power. They were facing double-digit infla-
tion and 16 percent interest rates, and the Republicans
were right on that. They have a very strong appeal to the
middle class on that issue. That is, conservatives are able
to take the abuses of the system—which cause people to
be insecure—and use that to evoke a conservative response from them.

DB: Do you see the left as a coherent political force in the country, or do you see it splintered?

It's a diverse force. It's issue-oriented. I don't see it splintered. People on Issue A have sympathy for people who work on Issue B. The political organizations are often splintered. I've heard people complain: why must we have six different groups doing solidarity work on El Salvador? Why couldn't they coalesce into one? We've seen unity on the nuclear war issue. SANE and the Nuclear Freeze have joined together into SANE/Freeze.

DB: They don't seem to build bridges to other issues, though. The issue, for example, of Palestinian self-determination does not seem to be very urgent for the left.

That may be true. To the extent that anybody's given any publicity to the plight of the Palestinians, it's been people on the left, but you may be right. I think what a lot of people on the left don't do is see the connection between these issues. The same people who are bringing us a militaristic and imperialist Israel are bringing us the first-strike and Star Wars and the escalation of nuclear weapons. They're the same people who are bringing us the dope inflow into the inner cities, the collaboration with the drug racketeers, the war in Central America. It's all connected. That's why you have to move from a liberal complaint to a radical analysis and see that you're dealing with class issues here and make a class analysis.

DB: If I may, what are your intentions? What are you trying to accomplish by your public talks, by your writings?

I'm trying to get people to see how all these issues are linked, to get them to see how the people who do the bad things they do don't do them because they're confused or stupid. The rulers know very well what they're doing.

They are rational actors pursuing rational interests, as
most people are in society. They may make mistakes, they
may suffer confusions, they may suffer defeats, they may
have differences of opinion among themselves, but they
generally know what they're doing and they know who
their enemies are, and their enemies are the people, the
people at home and the people abroad. Their enemies are.
anybody who wants more social justice, anybody who
wants to use the surplus value of society for social needs
rather than for individual class greed, that's their enemy.
My goal is to try to get people away from saying, "Isn't it
terrible how this goes on, what a strange foolish creature
man is?" and point out to them that most of us aren't
strange or foolish. We don't want these kind of things to
go on. These things are the product of a particular kind of
social organization and a particular use of class power.

Tools of the Trade

Language in the Service of Propaganda

Noam Chomsky

December 1, 1984

DB: Could you discuss the relationship between politics and language?

There is a tenuous relationship, in fact several different kinds. I think myself that they're exaggerated in importance. There is in the first place the question discussed, for example, by Orwell and by a number of others of how language is abused, tortured, distorted, in a way, to enforce ideological goals. A classic example would be the switch in the name of the Pentagon from the War Department to the Defense Department in 1947. As soon as that happened, any rational person should have understood that the United States would no longer be engaged in defense. It would only be engaged in aggressive war. That was essentially the case, and it was part of the reason for the change in terminology, to disguise that fact. One can go on to give innumerable examples of that sort. Perhaps the classic discussion of it is Orwell's *Politics and the English Language*.

There's also a more subtle and more interesting but even more tenuous connection which has to do with the fact that any stance that one takes with regard to social issues, for example, advocacy of some kind of reform or advocacy of a revolutionary change, an institutional change, or advocacy of stability and maintaining structures as they are—any such position, assuming that it has any moral basis at all and is not simply based on personal self-interest, is ultimately based on some conception of human nature. That is, if you suggest things should be reformed in this or that fashion and there's a moral basis for it, you are in effect saying, "Human beings are so constituted that this change is to their benefit. It somehow relates to their essential human needs." The underlying concept of human nature is rarely articulated. It's more or less tacit and implicit and nobody thinks about it very much. But if we were ever to achieve the state—and we're very far from this—if the study of humans were ever to reach the point of a discipline with significant intellectual content, this concept would have to be understood and articulated. If we search our souls we find that we do have a concept and it's probably based on some ideas about the underlying and essential human need for freedom from external arbitrary constraints and controls, a concept of human dignity which would regard it as an infringement on fundamental human rights to be enslaved, owned by others, in my view even to be rented by others, as in capitalist societies, and so on. Those views are not established at the level of science. They're just commitments. They could be issues of scientific investigation, that is, humans are what they are just as birds are what they are, you could find out what they are. At this point, the study of language may have some indirect relation, since it ultimately it does investigate some fundamental components of human intelligence and their nature and is at least suggestive of what human cognitive faculties are ultimately like, in fact it's more than suggestive about that. One might draw some tenuous speculations about other aspects of human nature of a sort that I mentioned with regard to freedom from external constraints, to subordination to external power, etc. But that's a real long distance, a hope for the future more than any present reality.

DB: Is freedom a linguistic imperative?

Just a superficial and obvious fact about human language is that it has an essentially creative aspect to it. Every normal human, independently of what we call "intelligence," over a huge range, apart from really severe pathology, quickly and with amazing rapidity, acquires a linguistic system which enables them to express and create new thoughts and to interact with others who also are creating and expressing new thoughts and to do it without bounds, though in a highly constrained fashion in terms of a rule system that's relatively fixed in its character as part of essential human nature, but that does permit and facilitate free creative expression. That's a fundamental aspect about human intelligence. It apparently differentiates humans from any other organism that we know about. How much that extends to other domains is an area of speculation but I think one can make some interesting guesses.

DB: Could you address the notion that words, language, have inherent power, concepts convey meaning beyond their words? What is happening mechanically when certain phrases are used, such as "the free world" or "strategic interests" or "national interests"?

That's the usual topic that's discussed when people talk about politics and language, and I think it's worth discussing, but I think it's almost obvious to the point of banality. Terms like "the free world" and "the national interest" and so on are mere terms of propaganda. One shouldn't take them seriously for a moment. They are designed, often very consciously, in order to try to block thought and understanding. For example, about the 1940's there was a decision, probably a conscious decision, made in public-relations circles to introduce terms like "free enterprise" and "free world" and so on instead of the conventional descriptive terms like "capitalism". Part of the reason was to insinuate somehow that the systems of

control and domination and aggression to which those
with power were committed here were in fact a kind of
freedom. That's just vulgar propaganda exercises. We are
inundated with this every moment of our lives. Many of
us internalize it, one has to defend oneself against it, but
once one realizes what's going on it's not very hard to do.
These are ways in which our intellects are dulled and our
capacity for thought is destroyed and our possibility for
meaningful political action is undermined by very effective systems of indoctrination and thought control that
involve, as all such systems do, abuse of language. One
can see this everywhere.

DB: You have written, "Among the many symbols
used to frighten and manipulate the populace of democratic states, few have been more important than terror
and terrorism." Could you talk about that?

For example, for the last several years, something
called "international terrorism" has been right at the front
of the agenda. There are conferences about it, books,
articles, etc. We were told when the Reagan administration came in that the struggle against international
terrorism was going to be the centerpiece of their foreign
policy, and it's continued that way. People debate as if
they were in the real world. They're not in the real world.
There is such a thing as international terrorism, and the
United States is one of the main sponsors of it. For
example, according to the official doctrine, the one that we
discuss and the one that George Schultz talks about, Cuba
is one of the main centers of international terrorism. The
propaganda literature on this topic, meaning people like
Claire Sterling and Walter Laqueur and others, basically
commissars, even argues that the proof that the communists are behind it all is that terrorism is in the so-called
"free world." The fact of the matter is that Cuba has been
subjected to more international terrorism than probably

the rest of the world put together. This began in the early 1960's when the Kennedy administration launched a major terrorist war against Cuba. It went on for many years; for all we know it's still going on. There's very little reporting on it. You have to work hard to find out what's going on from memoirs and participants' reports and so on. What has happened is a level of international terrorism that as far as I know has no counterpart, apart from direct aggression. It's included attacking civilian installations, bombing hotels, sinking fishing vessels, destroying petrochemical installations, poisoning crops and livestock, on quite a significant scale, assassination attempts, actual murders, bombing airplanes, bombing of Cuban missions abroad, etc. It's a massive terrorist attack. But this never appears in the discussions of international terrorism. Or, for example, take the Middle East. The very symbol of terrorism is the PLO, what could be more an example of terrorism? The PLO has certainly been involved in terrorist acts, but Israel, which is our client, has been involved in far greater, incomparably greater terrorist acts, except that we don't call them terrorist acts. For example, in the spring of this year, four young Palestinians in the Gaza Strip, who live under conditions of extreme oppression, hijacked a bus and tried to drive it out of the Gaza Strip. They apparently didn't have weapons, the bus was stopped by Israeli soldiers and in the fire they killed an Israeli woman on the bus. The soldiers knew that the bus was hijacked because these Palestinians had allowed a pregnant woman to leave the bus, who then informed them, as a humanitarian act on their part. The people who hijacked the bus were captured. Two were killed at once and two were taken away and murdered, apparently after torture by Israeli soldiers. That's all described as an act of Palestinian terrorism. There was an investigation of the murder of the two Palestinians by the Israeli army but nothing ever came of it, there's been no prosecution. About the same time, Israel bombed an area in Baalbek in Lebanon. According to the press reports, including American press reports, there were about 400 casualties, including approximately 150 children who were killed or wounded in an attack which destroyed a schoolhouse. That wasn't regarded as terrorism. Nobody ever referred to that as a terrorist act paid for by the United States, because of course they used American jets. That's just called an "unwise retaliatory strike" or something of that kind. This goes all the way back to the early 1970's, which was the high point of Palestinian terror attacks, and they were terror attacks, as in Maalot, etc. At that point, Israel was carrying out extensive bombardment of civilian targets in southern Lebanon to the extent that they actually drove out several hundred thousand people. That was never called terrorism. To use the term "double standard" for our approach is to really abuse the term, it goes beyond anything that you could call a double standard. It's almost a kind of fanaticism. It's a reflection of the extreme success of indoctrination in American society. You don't have any other society where the educated classes, at least, are so effectively indoctrinated and controlled by a propaganda system.

DB: Let's talk about that propaganda system. You've referred many times to the "state propaganda apparatus." What role do the media play in promoting and serving state interests?

One should be clear that in referring to the "state propaganda apparatus" here I do not mean that it comes from the state. Our system differs strikingly from, say, the Soviet Union, where the propaganda system literally is directed and controlled by the state. We're not a society which has a Ministry of Truth which produces doctrine which everyone then must obey at a severe cost if you don't. Our system works much differently and much more effectively. It's a privatized system of propaganda, including the media, the journals of opinion and in general including the broad participation of the articulate intelligentsia, the educated part of the population. The more articulate elements of that groups, the ones who have access to the media, including intellectual journals, and who essentially control the educational apparatus, they should properly be referred to as a class of "commissars." That's their essential function: to design, propagate and create a system of doctrines and beliefs which will undermine independent thought and prevent understanding and analysis of institutional structures and their functions. That's their essential social role. I don't mean to say they're conscious of it. In fact, they're not. In a really effective system of indoctrination the commissars are quite unaware of it and believe that they themselves are independent, critical minds. If you investigate the actual productions of the media, the journals of opinion, etc. you find exactly that. You find a very narrow, very tightly constrained and grotesquely inaccurate account of the world in which we live. The cases I mentioned in point are examples. There has never been more lively and extended debate in the United States, to my knowledge, than occurred over the war in Vietnam. Nevertheless, except for the very margins at the outside, the debate was entirely between those who were called "doves" and "hawks." Both the doves and the hawks began by accepting a lie so astonishing that Orwell couldn't have imagined it, namely the lie that we were defending South Vietnam when we were in fact attacking South Vietnam. Once you begin with that premise, everything else follows. Pretty much the same is true right now. Let's take the recent flap about the MIG's in Nicaragua. What was happening? The United States is sending advanced aircraft to El Salvador so that we are able to step up our attack on the population of El Salvador. The army that's carrying out this attack is really an occupying army, just like the Polish army is an occupying army of Poland, supported by a foreign power, except that the one in El Salvador is far more brutal and carrying out vastly more atrocities. We are trying to step up this attack by sending advanced aircraft and American pilots are now directly participating in controlling air strikes, etc. It's perfectly natural, any student of Orwell would expect, that we would accuse the other side of bringing in advanced aircraft. We're also conducting a real war against Nicaragua through a mercenary army. They're called "guerrillas" in the press, but they're nothing like any guerrilla army that's ever existed. They're armed at the level of a Central American army. They often outgun the Nicaraguan army. They're completely supplied and controlled by a foreign power. They have very limited indigenous support, as far as anybody knows. It's a foreign mercenary army attacking Nicaragua, using Nicaraguan soldiers, as is often the case in imperial wars. In this context, the big discussion is whether the Nicaraguans did or did not bring in aircraft which they could use to defend themselves. The doves say they probably didn't bring them in and therefore it was exaggerated. The doves also say, and here you can quote them, Paul Tsongas, for example, or Christopher Dodd, the most dovish Senators in Congress, that if indeed the Nicaraguans did bring in jets, then we should bomb them, because they would be a threat to us. When one looks at this, one sees something almost indescribable. Fifty years ago we heard Hitler talking about Czechoslovakia as a dagger pointed at the heart of Germany and people were appalled. But Czechoslovakia was a real threat to Germany as compared with the threat the Nicaragua poses to the United States. If we heard a discussion like this in the Soviet Union, where people were asking whether, let's say, Denmark should be bombed because it has jets which could reach the Soviet Union, we would be appalled. In fact, that's an analogy that's unfair to the Russians. They're not attacking Denmark as we're attacking Nicaragua and El Salvador. But here we accept it all. We accept it because the educated classes, the ones who are in a position, through prestige, privilege, education, etc., to present an intelligible understanding of the world, are so subordinated to the doctrinal system that they can't even see that two plus two equals four. They cannot see what's right in front of their eyes: that we are attacking Nicaragua and El Salvador and that of course the Nicaraguans have every right to defend themselves against our attack. If the Soviet Union had a mercenary army attacking Denmark, carrying out terrorist acts and trying to destroy the country, Denmark would have a right to defend itself. We would agree with that. When a comparable thing happens in our domains, the only thing we ask is, are they or are they not bringing in planes to defend themselves? If they are then we have a right to attack them even more. That assumption is essentially across the board. There's virtually no voice in the press which questions our right to take even more violent action against Nicaragua if they're doing something serious to defend themselves. That's an indication of a highly brainwashed society. By our standards Hitler looked rather sane in the 1930's.

DB: Let's talk a bit further about language and politics, specifically in the case of Nicaragua. The United States' Ambassador to Costa Rica was quoted in the *New York Times* as saying that "The Nicaraguan government has an extreme left network working for them in Washington. This is the same network that worked against American interests in Vietnam. It's sad to say that many Congressmen are prisoners of their own staffs, who rely on a preponderance of information from the left." The Ambassador then likens Nicaragua to Nazi Germany, and he makes this final statement that I'd particularly like you to address: "Nicaragua has become just like an infected piece of meat attracting these insects from all over," the insects being Libyans, Basque separatists, Cubans, the PLO, etc.

All of this is very reminiscent of Nazi Germany. The Ambassador's remarks are very typical of those produced by the Nazi diplomats at the same point, even in their style, the talk about "insects" and so on. Of course, what he describes is so remote from reality that it's superfluous even to discuss it. The idea of a leftist network in Washington is hilarious. What he would call "leftists" are people like Tsongas and Dodd. Those are precisely the kind of people he's referring to. The people who say that we should bomb Nicaragua if they do something to defend themselves. That's what to the Ambassador is a leftist attempting to undermine our policy. This is like a discussion of true Nazi propaganda, which doesn't even make a pretense of being related to reality and regards any deviation as unacceptable. We have to have total conformity, from his view, to the position that we are permitted and justified in carrying out any act of subversion, aggression, torture, murder, etc., and any deviation from that position is, from his point of view, a leftist conspiracy directed from Moscow. This is the extreme end of the propaganda system, and in fact it's not the important part, in my view. It's so crazy that anybody can see through it. The important part is the kind that doesn't seem so crazy, the kind that's presented by the doves, who ultimately accept not dissimilar positions. They accept the principle that we do have the right to use force and violence to undermine other societies that threaten our interests, which are the interests of the privileged, not the interests of the population. They accept that position and they discuss everything in those terms. Hence our attack against another country becomes "defense" of that country. Hence an effort by Nicaragua to acquire jets to defend itself becomes an unacceptable act that should evoke further violence on our part. It's that apparently critical position that plays the most significant role in our propaganda system. That's a point that's often not recognized. I think it's clearer if it's something that's a little more remote, so that we're not

directly engaged in it now. Let's take the Vietnam War.
The major contribution to the doctrinal system during the
Vietnam War period, in my view, is certainly the position
of the doves. The doves were saying that we were defending South Vietnam, that's just a given, but that it was
unwise, that it was costing too much, that it was beyond
our capacity and beyond our power. If we're capable of
thinking, we'll see that their position is very much like
that of Nazi generals after Stalingrad, who said it was a
mistake to get into a two-front war, and we probably won't
carry it off, and this is probably an effort that should be
modified and changed, though it is of course just and right.
We don't consider the Nazi generals doves. We recognize
what they are. But in a society in which that position is
considered to be the dissenting, critical position, in that
society the capacity for thought has been destroyed. It
means the entire spectrum of thinkable thoughts is now
caught within the propaganda system. It's the critics who
make the fundamental contribution to this. They are the
ones who foreclose elementary truth, elementary analysis, independent thought by pretending and being regarded as adopting a critical position, whereas in fact they
are subordinated to the fundamental principles of the
propaganda system. In my view that's a lot more important than the really lunatic comments that you just
quoted.

DB: What can people do to cut through this elaborate
and ornamented framework of propaganda and get at
what is real, get at the truth?

I frankly don't think that anything more is required
than ordinary common sense. What one has to do is adopt
towards one's own institutions, including the media and
the journals and the schools and colleges, the same rational, critical stance that we take towards the institutions
of any other power. For example, when we read the

productions of the propaganda system in the Soviet Union or Nazi Germany, we have no problem at all in dissociating lies from truth and recognizing the distortions and perversions that are used to protect the institutions from the truth. There's no reason why we shouldn't be able to take the same stance towards ourselves, despite the fact that we have to recognize that we're inundated with this, constantly, day after day. A willingness to use one's own native intelligence and common sense to analyze and dissect and compare the facts with the way in which they're presented is really sufficient. If the schools were doing their job, which of course they aren't, but they could be, they would be providing people with means of intellectual self-defense. They would be devoting themselves with great energy and application to precisely the kinds of things we're talking about so that people growing up in a democratic society would have the means of intellectual self-defense against the system. That means that individuals have to somehow undertake this task themselves. I don't think it's really very hard. I think once one perceives what is happening and is willing to take the first step of adopting a stance that is simply one of critical intelligence towards everything you read, in this morning's newspaper or tomorrow's newspaper or whatever and discover the assumptions that underlie it, analyze those assumptions, restate the account of the facts in terms that really are true to the facts, not simply reflections of the distorting prism of the propaganda system. Once one does that I think the world becomes rather clear. Then one can become a free individual, not merely a slave of some system of indoctrination and control.

DB: Could you talk about the twentieth century nation-state? I know you've written extensively about it. What is it in its makeup that permits first genocide, and now what Edward Said called in an article in *Harper's* the "phenomenon of refugees." Are these phenomena of the

twentieth century nation-state? Would you accept those
assumptions?

I don't entirely. I think there's some truth to it,
simply because the modern nation-state and the European model, that is, including the United States, happened to be by historical standards enormously powerful.
The degree of power in the hands of a modern nation-state
is something with no historical parallel. This power is
centrally controlled to a very high extent with a very
limited degree of popular participation in how that power
is exercised. Also, we have an awesome increase in the
level of power in the hands of the state, and as a result we
have an enormous amount of violence. However, it's very
misleading to think of, say, genocide as being a twentieth
century phenomenon. Let's just take our own history, the
history of the conquest of the Western Hemisphere. We
celebrate every year, at least in Massachusetts, we have
a holiday called "Columbus Day," and very few people are
aware that they're celebrating one of the first genocidal
monsters of the modern era. That's exactly what Columbus was. It's as if in Germany they would celebrate "Hitler
Day." When the colonists from Spain and England and
Holland and so on came to the Western Hemisphere, they
found flourishing societies. Current anthropological work
indicates that the number of native people in the Western
Hemisphere may have approached something like 100
million, maybe about 80 million south of the Rio Grande
and 12 million or so north of the Rio Grande. Within about
a century, that population had been destroyed. Take just
north of the Rio Grande, where there were maybe 10 or
12 million native Americans. By 1900 there were about
200,000, and most of them were killed off very quickly. In
the Andean region and Mexico there were very extensive
Indian societies, maybe something like 80 million people
throughout the southern part of the continent south of the
Rio Grande, and they're mostly gone. Many of them were

just totally murdered or wiped out, others succumbed to
European-brought diseases. This is massive genocide, and
that's long before the emergence of the twentieth century
nation-state. It may be one of the most, if not the most
extreme example from history, but far from the only one.
These are facts that we don't recognize. And the ways in
which we protect ourselves from these facts are often quite
astonishing. Let me give you a personal example. This
past Thanksgiving, last week, my family was here. We
went for a walk in a national park not far from here. We
came across a gravestone which had on it an inscription,
placed by the National Parks as a testimonial, in fact as
a gesture, no doubt conceived as a liberal gesture toward
the Indians in the past: "Here lies an Indian woman, a
Wampanoag, whose family and tribe gave of themselves
and their land that this great nation might be born and
grow." That is so appalling that one doesn't even know
how to discuss it. She and her family didn't "give of
themselves and their land," rather they were murdered
by our forefathers and driven out of their land. It's as if
200 years from now you came to Auschwitz and found a
gravestone saying, "Here lies a Jewish woman. She and
her family gave of themselves and their possessions so
that this great nation might grow and prosper." These
things are so appalling one doesn't even know how to
describe them. But these are reflections of what is regarded here as a liberal, accommodating, forthcoming
attitude. That's what's appalling and frightening. For
example, the very fact that we celebrate Columbus Day is
appalling. All of these aspects of our historical experience,
of the foundations of our own society, we are protected
from seeing. Sometimes when they are described they are
described in these unimaginable appalling ways. Again,
these are all aspects of the system of indoctrination to
which we are subjected. Looking at that gravestone, any
person of even minimal common sense and just the most
elementary knowledge of history should be totally ap-

palled. But person after person passes it by and thinks it's fine. It's again an indication of a level of indoctrination which is quite frightening.

DB: This raises the question of who controls history in our society.

History is owned by the educated classes. There are the people who are the custodians of history. They are the ones who are in universities and throughout the whole system of constructing, shaping and presenting to us the past as they want it to be seen. These are groups that are closely associated with power. They themselves have a high degree of privilege and access to power. They share class interests with those who control and in fact own the economic system. They are the cultural commissars of the system of domination and control that's very pervasive. I'm avoiding nuances. There are important exceptions. There are people who write honest history. But the point I'm describing is something that is overwhelmingly dominant, to the extent that only specialists would be likely to know things that fall outside it. For the ordinary citizen, one that doesn't have the resources or the time or the training or the education to really dig into things deeply on their own, the position they're presented with is the one I've described. For example, you can have a gravestone like that. That's why we can talk about genocide as a twentieth-century phenomenon, failing to recognize what happened not too far back in our own past.

DB: Could you talk about what is called "the first genocide of the twentieth century," which occurred in 1915 in Ottoman Turkey to the Armenians. Why is that a virtually unknown event? Why is that relegated to the periphery of our awareness?

Essentially because people had very little interest in it at the time. What happened is that something between several hundred thousand, maybe over a million people, were massacred in a quite short time. It was in Turkey, remote, no direct interest to Westerners, and hence they paid very little attention to it. I think much more dramatic and striking is the fact that comparable genocidal acts which are much closer to us, and in fact in which we have been directly involved, are suppressed. For example, I would wager that more people are aware of the Armenian genocide during the First World War than are aware of the Indonesian genocide in 1965 when 700,000 people were massacred within a couple of months. That was with the support of the United States. It was greeted with polite applause in the United States because it "returned Indonesia to the free world," as we described it at the time. That genocide was used, including by American liberals, I should say, as justification for our war in Indochina. It was described as having provided a "shield" behind which these delightful events could take place. That's a much more striking fact than our casual attitude towards a genocidal attack on the Armenians 70 years ago.

DB: That connects directly with a two-volume set that you co-authored with Edward Herman, *The Washington Connection and Third World Fascism* and *After the Cataclysm*. You talk extensively about the events in 1965 in Indonesia and then the events in 1975, in East Timor...

Which are still going on, incidentally. There's a case of genocide that's going on right today and is continuing precisely because the United States supports it. That's what blocks any possible termination of that genocidal attack. There's one right in front of our eyes for which we're directly responsible and there's virtually no awareness of it. I doubt if one person in 100 in the United States ever even heard of Timor [East Timor was a former Portuguese colony].

DB: Why is that? Does it serve some ideological interest that there's no information?

Sure. It's quite improper for people in the United States to know that their own government is involved in a genocidal massacre which is quite comparable to Pol Pot. Therefore they better not know about it, and they don't. This is particularly striking because it began, as you say, in 1975, just at the time that the Pol Pot massacres began. They're rather comparable in many ways, except that the Timorese massacre was carried out by an invading army rather than being a peasant revolution taking revenge and controlled by a gang of fanatics who were carrying out huge massacres in their own society. These two are rather comparable in scale. Relative to the population, in fact, the Timorese massacre is maybe two or three times as great, once all the propaganda is filtered away and we look at the actual facts. The treatment of them was quite different. The Pol Pot massacres received enormous attention, tremendous protest, this was compared to the Nazis. The Timorese massacre, that we were responsible for, was suppressed. People went way out of their way to try to find Cambodian refugees on the Thai-Cambodian border so that they could tell horror stories. They didn't go to Lisbon, which is much easier to reach than the Thai-Cambodian border, to talk to Timorese refugees who would tell them what the United States was backing in Timor. That whole near-genocidal attack, the term is not exaggerated in this case, was almost entirely suppressed for over four years. Even today it's barely discussed, and when it is discussed, the American role is suppressed. For example, the *New York Times* finally began to talk about it and ran editorials, one was called "The Shaming of Indonesia." Sure, it's the shaming of Indonesia, but it's also the shaming of the United States. We're the ones who blocked every diplomatic effort to stop it. The Carter administration, which was supposedly committed to human rights, vastly increased the flow of arms to Indonesia with the certain knowledge that they were going to be used to extend the massacre in East Timor, there was nothing else that they could be used for. None of this is the shaming of the United States, nor is it the shaming of the *New York Times* that they didn't report it for four years, even today aren't reporting what's going on. These are again ways of protecting ourselves from understanding of the world in which we live and function as agents. The population has to be protected from any understanding of that. That's one of the main purposes of the indoctrination system, to prevent the population from understanding what they are participating in indirectly through the institutions that they support.

DB: And one sees, for example, in the case of the massacre and ongoing killings in East Timor, a certain sense of bipartisanship. It started under the Ford administration in 1975, it continued during the Carter years...

It escalated during the Carter years.

DB: ...and is continuing during the Reagan period.

The worst period was the Carter period, and it's still continuing now. Last year there was another major Indonesian offensive. Once again the Red Cross has been withdrawn, so there's virtually no international observation. About the only information we're getting is from refugees and the Catholic church. The church has been reporting these atrocities, but that virtually never reaches an American audience. We should ask ourselves, why are our institutions so concerned to prevent us from knowing what we're doing? I think the reason for that is that the people in power are simply afraid of the population. What they're afraid of is if the general population has any awareness and understanding of what the state is up to, they'll protest and they'll stop it. That's why we have these extremely elaborate and very effective systems of thought control. Why don't they just tell us the truth? They don't tell us the truth because they're afraid of us. They're afraid that if we know we're going to stop them. Hence the lies. Hence the educational system. Hence the media. And so on.

DB: Let's talk about what I reluctantly call "censorship." Perhaps you can find a better word for it here in the United States. Earlier I mentioned the two-volume set that you have co-authored with Edward Herman, *The Washington Connection* and *After the Cataclysm.* Correct me if I'm mistaken, but I believe that neither of those books received any prominent media coverage or book reviews, and now you have a new book with the title *The Fateful Triangle* which has only received two reviews. One can draw two conclusions: Either the books are indeed terrible and not worth writing about, or perhaps a more cynical point of view would be that there's some kind of censorship being exercised here.

As to whether they're worth writing about, obviously I think so or I wouldn't have written them. We can make a kind of objective test of that. For example, we can ask how the same books are received in other societies similar to ours. Take, say, Canada. Canada is a country very similar to the United States and has essentially the same values, institutions, social organizations, etc. Kind of like an adjunct to the United States. But as soon as we cross the border, we find that the treatment of these books and their authors is radically different than it is here. For example, *The Fateful Triangle,* which came out about a year ago, is primarily concerned with American policy. It's peripheral to the interests of Canadians, but central to the interests of Americans. It was barely mentioned in the press here, and is very hard to find. You have to really work to dig it out somewhere. It's probably not in the libraries. But in Canada it was radically different. It was reviewed in major journals. It was reviewed in most minor journals, even in the *Financial Post,* which is sort of like the *Wall Street Journal.* It was reviewed in the news weeklies, the equivalent of *Time* and *Newsweek.* Every time I go to Canada I'm immediately on Canadian radio and television. I was there last week for a day, and I had three interviews on national CBC. In the United States, it's radically different. People with similar views, not just me, are marginalized, excluded, no reviews, no purchases of books, individuals can do it, but you rarely find such books in the libraries, media almost totally closed off. If we look at other countries similar to the United States, the same is true. In England and Australia, again countries very much like us, these books are reviewed, discussed, etc. Not in the United States, however. If the judgment is one of quality, then it's striking that the judgment is so different across the border. Incidentally, many of the reviews are quite critical, but that's fair enough. People say what they think.

DB: Could you speculate why, for example, you're not on occasionally Dan Rather's *CBS Evening News* or National Public Radio's *All Things Considered.* Has Noam Chomsky been marginalized, to use the very term that you've coined?

That's always been the case. For example, during the Vietnam War, when I was very visible in opposition to the war on the international scene and here too, I live in Boston and I was constantly in the radio and television studios here. But for foreign interviews. I think I was once on public radio in the Boston area during the Vietnam War. I had just returned from a trip to Indochina and I was on for about five minutes. But I was constantly on Australian, Canadian, British, continental European radio and television. That's constantly the case. Just in the last few weeks I've been on national Italian television, on Canadian television, on Irish radio, all over the place. In another couple of weeks I'm going to England for a day for a big television program discussing politics. This is constant and common. In the United States it's virtually unknown. In fact it's very striking that I'm now talking over a Colorado radio station. When you get out of the main centers in the United States, out of New York, Boston and Washington, then the controls ease. For example, if I go to Denver or Boulder or Des Moines or Minneapolis or San Diego, then it's not at all unlikely that I'll be asked to talk on political topics on radio and sometimes television. But in the main ideological centers it's unimaginable. Again, that's not just me, it's other people who are essentially dissenting critics. This reflects the sophistication of our ideological system. What happens in areas that are marginal with respect to the exercise of power doesn't matter so much. What happens in the centers of power matters a great deal. Therefore the controls are tighter to the extent that you get closer to the center. As soon as you cross the border to Canada nobody really cares much what happens, so therefore it's much freer.

DB: So essentially if, as you did last year, you come to Boulder and give many public lectures and appear on KGNU and now doing a phone interview on KGNU, that's OK since we're out here in the boondocks, as it were.

It's not totally OK, but it's better. It could never happen on National Public Radio. [On March 30, 1988 Noam Chomsky was interviewed for the first time on National Public Radio's *All Things Considered.*]

DB: One final question, about George Orwell. I sense from your writing and from some of the comments you've made in this interview that you feel a certain kinship with Orwell. Have you been influenced by him at all?

It's a little complicated. I think Orwell wrote one really great book which did influence me a lot. That was *Homage to Catalonia.* This is the book that he wrote about his experiences during the Spanish Civil War in the late 1930's. The history of that book is itself interesting and revealing. That book appeared in 1937. It was not published in the United States. It was published in England, and it sold a couple hundred copies. The reason that the book was suppressed was because it was critical of communists. That was a period when pro-communist intellectuals had a great deal of power in the intellectual establishment. It's similar to the kind of control that many people called "pro-Israel," although I think it's a bad term, but people who are called "pro-Israel" have over media and expression today. They're similar in many respects. They succeeded in preventing Orwell's book from appearing. It did appear about 10 years later, and it appeared as a Cold War tract because it was anti-Russian and fashions had changed. That was a really important book. I think there were things wrong with it, but I think it was a book of real great significance and importance. It's probably the least known of Orwell's major political books. His better-known books in my view are not very significant. For example, *1984,* which is very popular here, in fact it's a major bestseller, because it can be easily construed as anti-Russian propaganda. But it's a very shallow book, basically. Orwell was giving a satirical analysis based upon existing Soviet society. Existing Soviet society and its terror have been very well described by factual analyses not very well known here, but they existed. People like Maximov, for example, the anarchist historian, had given excellent detailed analyses of Leninist and Stalinist institutionalized terror going back to the Revolution. You didn't have to go to Orwell and fantasy to find this out. Orwell's

fictionalized account was in my view no major contribution and also not very well done. I think it's a really
tenth-rate novel. We also tend to suppress some of the
aspects of it. He was also talking about England, not just
Russia. He was talking about what he expected to happen
in the industrial democracies, and as a prediction that was
very bad, that hasn't happened. I also think he missed the
main techniques of thought control and indoctrination in
the democracies. For example, in England and the United
States we do not use for control the devices he described,
crude vicious use of highly visible power. That's not the
way thought control works here. It works by much more
subtle and much more effective devices, the kinds we've
been talking about. Orwell completely missed this. So I
think that *1984* is very much overrated. On the other
hand, he was an honest man. He did try to, and often
succeeded, in extricating himself from the systems of
thought control, and in that respect he was very unusual
and very praiseworthy. But the one great book that he
wrote, in my view, is the one that I mentioned, *Homage to
Catalonia.*

   DB: Bernard Crick, who is a British biographer of
Orwell, seems to corroborate what you say. He suggests
that it is in Orwell's essays where "the dirty work of
imperialism is illuminated," such as "A Hanging" and
"Shooting an Elephant" that Orwell would be best remem-
bered and the earlier mentioned "Politics and the English
Language."

   I agree with that. The famous works are the least
significant.

Terrorism:
The Politics of Language

Noam Chomsky

October 24, 1986

DB: To what extent does the control of language shape and form our perceptions and understanding of reality?

There are obvious examples. One important fact to bear in mind when one listens to or is subjected to political discourse is that most terms are used in a kind of a technical meaning that's really very much divorced from their actual meaning, sometimes even the opposite of it. For example, take a term like "national interest." The term "national interest" is commonly used as if it's something good for us, and the people of the country are supposed to understand that. So if a political leader says that "I'm doing this in the national interest," you're supposed to feel good because that's for you. However, if you look closely, it turns out that the national interest is not defined as what's in the interest of the entire population; it's what's in the interests of small, dominant elites who happen to be able to command the resources that enable them to control the state—basically, corporate-based elites. That's what's called the "national interest." And, correspondingly, the term "special interests" is used in a very interesting related way to refer to the general population. The population are called the "special interests" and the corporate elite are called the "national interest"; so you're supposed to be in favor of the national interest and against the special interests.

This became very clear in the last few presidential campaigns. The Reagan administration is largely a figment of the public relations industry, and the public relations aspects of it, including control over language, are very striking—it's a professional public relations outfit. It was interesting to see how the choice of terms they use was carefully crafted. In both the 1980 and 1984 elections, they identified the Democrats as the "party of special interests," and that's supposed to be bad, because we're all against the special interests. But if you look closely and ask who were the special interests, they listed them: women, poor people, workers, young people, old people, ethnic minorities—in fact, the entire population. There was only one group that was not listed among the special interests: corporations. If you'll notice the campaign rhetoric, that was never a special interest, and that's right, because in their terms that's the *national* interest. So if you think it through, the population are the special interests and the corporations are the national interest, and since everyone's in favor of the national interest and against the special interests, you vote for and support someone who's against the population and is working for the corporations. This is a typical case of the way the framework of thought is consciously manipulated by an effective choice and reshaping of terminology so as to make it difficult to understand what's happening in the world. A very important function of the ideological institutions—the media, the schools, and so on—is to prevent people from perceiving reality, because if they perceived it they might not like it and might act to change it, and that would harm privileged people who control these things.

DB: Perhaps it's like George Orwell said in his essay "Politics and the English Language," that in our time political speech and writing is largely the "defense of the indefensible."

Yes, he gave interesting examples which are now classic, like the term "pacification." It is used for mass murder; thus we carried out "pacification" in Vietnam. If you look at what the pacification programs were, they were literally programs of mass murder to try to suppress and destroy a resisting civilization population. Orwell wrote long before Vietnam, but he already noted that pacification was being used that way; by now it's an industry. Orwell had pointed out early examples of this kind of usage. A standard example is "defense." In the United States, up until 1947, we used to have something called the "War Department." Since 1947, we haven't had a War Department; we've had a "Defense Department." Anyone who had his head screwed on realized in 1947 that we were not going to be involved in defense any more, we were only going to be involved in war, and that's why the War Department has to be renamed the Defense Department—because "defense" means "aggression." By now this is a sophisticated operation. It's the same with every term you can think of. Take the term "conservative." Conservative is supposed to be a good thing, and this is supposed to be a conservative administration. A true conservative like, say, Robert Taft, would turn over in his grave to see what's being called conservative. Everything the conservatives have always fought against is being advanced by this administration. This administration is in favor of extending the power of the state and increasing the intervention of the state in the economy. State power has increased faster under this administration than under any since the Second World War. It's also interested in protecting the state against its citizens, cutting down access to the state, controlling thought, controlling expression, attacking civil liberties, attacking individual rights. It's the most lawless administration we've ever had. All of these things are anathema to conservatives. Conservatives want the opposite in every respect, so naturally they call the administration conservative, and if you like it you're supposed to be conservative. These are all ways of undermining the possibility of independent thought, by eliminating even the tools that you can use to engage in it.

DB: Could you talk a little bit about the power of naming? That seems to be crucial in this whole process.

These are all examples of it. Language is, after all, a tool for thought. If you debase the language, you debase the thought. I don't want to exaggerate this element of it, but it is one element, and one that's certainly consciously manipulated in order to introduce confusion and lack of perception.

DB: It seems in recent years, certainly starting in the 1970s, through the 1980s and for the foreseeable future, the term "terrorism" has become a dominant issue, a theme and focus for the media and politicians, I wonder if you could talk about the word itself; it seems to have undergone a curious transformation in the last couple of centuries.

It definitely has, it's a very interesting case. The word "terrorism" came into general use at the end of the 18th century, and it was then used to refer to acts of violent states that suppressed their own populations by violence. Terror was the action of a state against its own citizens. That concept is of no use whatsoever to people in power, so, predictably, the term has come to be changed. Now it's the actions of citizens against states; in fact, the term "terrorism" is now almost entirely used for what you might call "retail terrorism": the terrorism of small, marginal groups, and not the terrorism of powerful states. We have one exception to this: if our enemies are involved in terrorism, then you can talk about "state terrorism." So there are really two things that define terrorism. First, it's done against states, not by states against their citizens, and it's done by them, not us. So, for example, take Libya. Qaddafi is certainly a terrorist. The latest edition of the Amnesty International publication, *Political Killings by Governments*, lists Qaddafi as a terrorist; he killed fourteen people, Libyans, mostly in Libya, in the 1980s. There may be a handful of others, but even taking the most extreme estimate it couldn't be more than several dozen, probably less. That's terrorism, and he's therefore the "Mad Dog of the Middle East" and the "King of International Terrorism." That's because he meets our criteria: he's them, not us, and the terrorism that one talks about is carried out generally by small groups, not by one of our major states.

Let's compare it with El Salvador. In the same years in which Libya killed maybe fourteen, maybe 20 people, mostly Libyans, the government of El Salvador slaughtered about 50,000 people. Now that's not just terrorism, that's international terrorism, because it was done by us. We instituted the government as much as the Russians instituted the government in Afghanistan; we created the army, a terrorist army; we supplied, organized and directed it. The worst atrocities were carried out by American-trained elite battalions fresh from their training. The U.S. Air Force participated directly in coordinating bombing strikes—the terror was not ordinary killing. Libyan terror is bad enough; they kill people. But our terrorists first mutilate, torture, rape, cut them to pieces—it's hideous torture, Pol Pot-style. That's not called terrorism. El Salvador is not called a terrorist state. José Napoléon Duarte—who has presided over all this, who has perceived his role from the beginning as ensuring that the murderers are supplied with weapons, and that nothing will interfere with the massacre which he knew was coming when he joined the military junta—he's called a great liberal hero, and El Salvador is considered a kind of magnificent triumph of democracy. Here's a major terrorist state—Libya is a very, very minor terrorist state—

but we see it the other way around, and the reason is
because "terrorism" is used for them, not us, and because
in the case of El Salvador it's plainly being done by a major
state against its own citizens—in fact a state that we
established, a client state of the United States. Therefore
it can't be terrorism, by definition. This is true in case after
case. My book about it, *Pirates and Emperors,* takes its
title from a rather nice story by St. Augustine in his *City
of God.* St. Augustine describes a confrontation between
King Alexander the Great and a pirate whom he caught.
Alexander the Great asks the pirate, "How dare you
molest the sea?" The pirate turns to Alexander the Great
and says, "How dare you molest the whole world? I have
a small boat, so I am called a thief and a pirate. You have
a navy, so you're called an emperor." St. Augustine con-
cludes that the pirate's answer was elegant and excellent
and that essentially tells the story. Retail terrorism directed against our interests is terrorism; wholesale terrorism carried out for our interests isn't terrorism.

The same is true in the Middle East region. In case
after case, this is the way the term is used, and very
effectively. In fact, it was very predictable that the Reagan
administration would take international terrorism to be
the core of its foreign policy, as it announced right off. The
reason was that the administration made it very clear that
it was going to be engaged in international terrorism on a
massive scale, and since it's going to be engaged in international terrorism, naturally, in a good public relations-
directed world, you start off by saying that you're opposed
to international terrorism. That shifts attention away
from the crucial issue: that you're going to maximize
international terrorism.

DB: Why the tremendous fascination with terrorism—the TV specials, the articles, the documentaries, the
symposia, the conferences, and on and on—is there something deeper that's being touched by this?

Oh, yes, very deep. It's very close to the Reagan administration's domestic policies. It's important to remember that the Reagan administration's policies are extremely unpopular, and for obvious reasons. The polls show this very clearly; on just about every major issue the public is strongly opposed to the Reagan programs. Take, say, social spending vs. military spending. When the question is asked in polls: Would you prefer to have a decrease in welfare payments or in military spending?, the overwhelming majority of the population supports social spending and opposes military spending. In fact, much of the population is quite willing to see taxes raised to improve social spending. The same is true on just about every issue. On intervention abroad (in other words, international terrorism, if we were to be honest), the population is strongly against it, by large majorities. The Reagan administration is for it. On the nuclear freeze, the public is overwhelmingly in favor of it; the figure is something like three to one. The administration is against it. And so on. As you go down the line, every major policy program is unpopular. This is a problem, of course; you've got to control the population. There is a classic answer to this problem: you frighten them.

Let me just go back to another step of the Reagan program which is even more obvious: an essential part of the Reagan program was to try to transfer resources from the poor to the rich. Now, that's going to be unpopular, and the attack on social spending is a part of it. Much of the Reagan program is turning an increasingly powerful state into a welfare state for the rich. The military program is very largely for that purpose. That's a forced public subsidy to advanced industry, again unpopular, and you can't present it in these terms. What do you do? You have to get the public lined up. They oppose your policies. There's only one way to deal with this; every leader throughout history has understood it. You've got to frighten them, make them think their lives are at stake, that they've got to defend themselves, and then they'll accept these programs that they despise or dislike as an unfortunate necessity. How do you terrify people? Again, there's a classic answer: you find some "Evil Empire" that's threatening to destroy them. In our case, it's now the Soviet Union; it used to be the Huns, before that, the British, and so on. But since the Bolshevik revolution it's been the Soviet Union that's threatening to destroy us. So that's the Evil Empire. But here you run into a problem. Confrontations with the Evil Empire are dangerous. That's a big, powerful state; it can fight back, and you don't want to get involved with them because you might get hurt. So what you have to do is have confrontations, but not with the Evil Empire—too dangerous. The best way is to have confrontations with groups that you designate as "proxies" of the Evil Empire. What you try to do is to find essentially defenseless countries or groups that can be attacked at will, and designate them to be proxies of the Evil Empire, and then you can defend yourself against them by attacking them. Libya, for example, is perfect for this purpose. It has loose associations with the Soviet Union. It's a minor actor in the world of international terrorism. Against the background of anti-Arab racism, which is rampant in the United States—it's the last legit-imate form of racism—you can easily talk about the Mad Dog and how he ought to get down from the trees and all this kind of stuff; that works, that scares people. Further-more, if you can manage to elicit terrorism, which some of our acts have done, that will really frighten people, since that strikes at home. In fact, actual terrorism is very slight; you're much more likely to be hit by lightning. But people can get scared, and a confrontation with Libya is cheap. You can kill Libyans at will; they can't fight back, it's a tiny, defenseless country, we can beat them up every time we feel like it. It will make people here feel that somehow our courageous cowboy leader is defending us from these monsters who are going to destroy us, most of

which is a public relations concoction. In fact, throughout
the history of the Reagan administration there has been
a sequence of carefully concocted, fraudulent incidents
created to give us an opportunity to attack and kill Libyans, always for some specific political purpose at home,
like building up support for the rapid deployment force,
an intervention force in the Middle East or gaining support for contra aid, or one thing or another. They're very
carefully timed, as I said; this is a public relations administration. Their genius is manipulation of the public;
that's what they're good at, and Libya is a perfect proxy
of the Evil Empire, as I say: you can kill them, you can
attack them, you can bomb them, people here can be
frightened enough to think that they're somehow being
defended by these terrorist attacks. That way, if people
feel sufficiently embattled, they'll support these programs
that they oppose. And they do. The spring of 1986, for
example, was a brilliant exercise in public relations—

DB: The bombing of Libya

—and the impact, the pretext for it was fabricated.
It was covered up by the media, which know the true story
but will not report it. It terrified the domestic population—people wouldn't even go to Europe, they were so
scared, which is ludicrous, you're a hundred times as safe
in any European city as in any American city—but people
were so terrified they stayed at home. That's wonderful,
because if you can terrify the domestic population then
they'll support things like Star Wars or whatever lunacy
comes along in the belief that you have to defend yourself.
Crucially, you can't have confrontations with the Russians; they can fight back. So you've got to find somebody
you can beat up at will: Grenada, Libya, Nicaragua, anybody who can't fight back, that's what you need. I should
say, incidentally, that this is understood very well abroad.
When you read the foreign press, they regularly comment

on the thuggishness and the cowardice of this administration, the sort of "bully on the block mentality": you find
somebody little enough to beat up and you go send your
goon squads to beat him up, that's essentially their style;
but here somehow people can't see it.

DB: This retail minor-actor terrorism you've been
talking about—when it's presented in the media it occurs
ahistorically: it has no context, it's totally irrational, so it
seems that the logical response would be one of loathing
and fear, and it's very effective.

That's right. Most of the retail terrorism—what is
called "terrorism" in the United States—comes out of
Lebanon, and that started in 1982. It was a very marginal
phenomenon before that, a major phenomenon, mainly in
Europe, after 1982; so plainly something must have happened in 1982 to cause terrorism to start coming out of
Lebanon. Well, yes, something happened in 1982: with
enthusiastic American support, Israel attacked Lebanon.
The purpose of the Israeli attack was to demolish the
civilian society of the Palestinians so as to ensure Israeli
control over the West Bank, and in the process it also
destroyed much of what was left of Lebanon. Lebanon was
left in ruins, the Palestinian community was destroyed,
and Lebanon, already in bad shape, got the final blow. The
United States supported it all the way. We vetoed U.N.
resolutions trying to stop the aggression, we supplied
Israel with arms, diplomatic support, the whole business,
and naturally it was perfectly predictable that that was
going to evoke international terrorism. You cut off every
political option for people and they are going to turn to
terrorism. And I should say that this was well understood
in Israel. Here you can't talk about it, because we're a
much more indoctrinated country, but in Israel, which is
a more democratic society—at least for the Jewish majority—this was openly discussed. For example, the current

prime minister, Yitzhak Shamir, pointed out that there
was a threat to Israel from the Palestinians, but said it
was a political, not a military threat. The threat was that
they would compel Israel to enter into a political settlement that it didn't want, and that had to be stopped.
Israel's and perhaps the world's leading specialist on the
Palestinians, a professor at Hebrew University named
Yehoshua Porath, wrote an analysis shortly after the
invasion, a long, detailed article in *Ha'aretz*, Israel's major
newspaper (kind of like Israel's *New York Times*), in which
he explained what he thought, very plausibly, the invasion was about. He said, and I'm paraphrasing: Look,
here's the situation. For the last year, the PLO has not
engaged in any cross-border terrorism. Israel has tried to
get them to do it, we have continually bombed them and
murdered them and so on to try to evoke some response
across the border, but they haven't done it. They've kept
discipline despite the fact that we've bombed them, killing
dozens of people and so forth. This is a veritable catastro-
phe for the Israeli leadership, since if the PLO continues
to maintain this posture of not engaging in cross-border
terrorism and demanding a diplomatic settlement, Israel
might be driven to a political settlement, which it does not
want because in a political settlement it would have to
give up control of the occupied territories. What the Israeli
leadership wants is to return the PLO to much earlier
days when it engaged in random terrorism, a PLO that
will hijack airplanes, kill many Jews and be a source of
loathing and horror throughout the world. They don't
want a peaceful PLO that refuses to respond to Israeli
terrorist attacks and insists on negotiation. That's what
the invasion will achieve.

Others also commented in the same way, and that's
a very plausible analysis. I presume that's what the plan-
ners in the Reagan administration wanted, too. From
their point of view, terrorism coming out of Lebanon is
very beneficial. It frightens the American population;

terrorist acts are indeed loathsome, and if you cut people off from every possible option, you can predict pretty well that that's what they're going to do. So let's take, for example, the Karachi hijacking. It appears—we don't know for sure—as if the hijackers were victims of the Sabra Shatila massacre. Everybody knows what that was. That's what happens—you send killers into a defenseless civilian area for the purpose of slaughtering and torturing people, and those who survive are very likely to turn to terrorism, and that's in effect what happened. People pretend they don't understand, but anyone who can look at dates can figure it out. The Lebanese-based terrorism, mainly in Europe, since 1982 is a direct, predictable and probably desired effect of the U.S.-backed Israeli aggression in Lebanon, which eliminated the hope of a political settlement, demolished the civilian society and the PLO— brutally, I should say—and smashed to pieces what was left of Lebanon; so that's what happens. And every time we look there's a context.

There's an interesting reaction here when this is brought up: "You're justifying terrorism." I'm not justifying terrorism; justification and explanation are two different things. What you're pointing out is that there's an explanation for terrorism, and if you want to stop it you look at the explanation. When you look at the explanation you quite often find that violent, powerful states try to evoke terrorism because it's in their interest. That's no justification; it's an explanation. Terrorist acts are indeed loathsome. It was loathsome when Leon Klinghoffer was thrown off a boat in a wheelchair and killed on October 7, 1985. It was also loathsome when, a week earlier, Israeli bombed Tunis and killed about 75 people using "smart" bombs that the United States probably supplied them. That's loathsome too. We regard one, but not the other, as terrorism, because one was wholesale terrorism on our side and the other was retail terrorism on their side.

DB: That particular attack, the Tunis bombing, is, of course, always framed in the concept of retaliation; it was a response, not initiated.

Every terrorist act is *always* called retaliation. The sequence is as follows: first came a PLO attack in Larnaca, Cyprus, where three Israelis were killed. The killers were immediately caught and placed on trial; they're now in jail. About a week later came the Israeli bombing of Tunis in which, according to Israeli correspondents, about 75 people were killed, 20 Tunisians and 55 Palestinians, mostly civilians. Then, a week after that came the Achille Lauro hijacking with the Klinghoffer assassination. All three of these things were called retaliations by the people who did them. The Larnaca, Cyprus operation was called a retaliation for a fact which is suppressed here, namely that the Israeli navy, apparently using agents based on Cyprus, has been hijacking boats for over ten years— that's called terrorism when the other guy does it—hijacking boats in transit between Cyprus and various parts of northern Lebanon. In fact, they have often taken Palestinians off those boats and handed them over to their own Maronite allies in Lebanon, who then killed them. The PLO claimed that Larnaca was in retaliation for the many years of hijacking, which certainly happened, there's no doubt. We didn't call that retaliation, we just called it terrorism. Then came the Israeli bombing, which they called retaliation, except with one slight problem: it was not directed against the people who carried out the terrorist attack. In fact, Israel had conceded that the people they were bombing in Tunis apparently had nothing to do with the Larnaca attack. But it was a cheap target. The people who had to do with the attack probably came from Syria, but that's not a cheap target; they can fight back. Tunis, on the other hand, is a defenseless target, so you attack it. That's the way it's done. It was done, incidentally, with the complicity of the United States, The U.S. Sixth Fleet in the Mediterranean certainly had the Israeli bombers under surveillance. They claimed they couldn't see them, which was ridiculous. The Israelis had to fly all the way across the Mediterranean; they were refueled in flight, they passed by the most sophisticated radar and surveillance systems that the U.S. government and military can establish, and somehow we claimed that they were invisible. That's nonsensical; we obviously knew they were coming, and we didn't warn Tunis. Tunis is a loyal American ally, but we didn't warn them that the killers were on the way. Anyhow, they called that a retaliation, but of course it wasn't. It had nothing to do with the attack. Then came the Achille Lauro hijacking. They called that a retaliation, namely for the Tunis bombing, and you can trace it back as far as you like, go back to the first interaction, and every step is called by the terrorists a retaliation for what came before, and in a certain sense it is. That's the cycle: repression, violence, retaliation, more retaliation, preemption, etc. In our ideological system, we have a very simple way to handle it. When the guys we don't like do it, it's terror. When the guys we do like do it, it's retaliation.

From *MacNeil-Lehrer* to *Nightline*

Experts Enforce the Party Line

Jeff Cohen

January 30, 1990

DB: In the October/November 1989 issue of *Extra,* you had an article talking about the notion of objectivity and balance and propaganda of the center. It's particularly this latter issue that I'd like to talk to you about, because propaganda seems to be a property of the left and the right, because we have objectivity at the center.

Right. When you've talked to journalists for years in the mainstream, they always tell you, "We have no biases. We're dead center. We're not left nor right." I think there is a commonly believed myth in the mainstream media that if you are a centrist you have no ideology. You issue no propaganda. You just issue straight news. The only people that are propagandists are propagandists for the right wing or the left wing. What Fairness and Accuracy in Reporting (FAIR) has been trying to bring forward to journalists is that, if you're in the center, your ideology is centrism, which is every bit as much an ideology as leftism or rightism. I've talked to journalists and they say, "We ward off propaganda from both left and right." And my question is always, "Well, who's warding off propaganda from the center? It tends to be most of the propaganda in at least the TV networks." They don't have a response. The propaganda for the center has certain hallmarks. One

thing about centrist propaganda is that it talks in euphe-
misms all the time. Anything that might strike at the core
of what's wrong with our corporate-dominated society is
always spoken of euphemistically. The way that centrist
propaganda looks at foreign policy is one where the United
States is always overseas making peace, trying to bring
opposing parties together, constantly trying to negotiate
and expand human rights. You find this in the *New York
Times,* which I think is the propaganda organ of the
center, where you had headlines about George Schulz as
the "lonely warrior for peace." This was during the period
where U.S. foreign policy was arming the UNITA guerrillas in Angola, who had turned central Angola into the
amputee capital of the world. You had the United States
funding the contras and the bulwark for the Salvadoran
government. And, of course, in the Middle East, where the
United States contributes hundreds of millions of dollars
to Israel. In all those places, when the *New York Times*
refers to foreign policy, it's as George Schulz or Baker
crusading for peace, trying to bring parties together. It's
not acknowledged that in those parts of the world the
United States is a major player in a violent conflict. That's
a hallmark of center propaganda. What I've found interesting and important is to distinguish what is left-wing
propaganda, what is right-wing propaganda and what is
middle-of-the-road propaganda. Left-wing propaganda
sees U.S. foreign policy as going overseas mostly in the
interests of corporations, propping up elites in foreign
countries that are anti-communist, not really concerned
whether those elites are at all democratic. The right-wing
propaganda in foreign policy sees the United States going
around generally being too soft on communism, caving in
to communism and terrorism. The center has its own view
of foreign policy, and that's the United States going
around the world bringing human rights, trying to expand
democracy and negotiate between warring parties. I
would argue that one could deconstruct centrist propa-

ganda and find that it has very little basis in fact. That's what we did in this article that you're referring to.

DB: In January 1989, FAIR issued a rather remarkable report about *Nightline*. You drew certain conclusions about the number of guests, who they were, the frequency of appearances, who they represented and that kind of thing. Has anything changed at *Nightline* since your report?

Things have changed only slightly, and they've changed in some cosmetic ways, but let me describe what we found. We studied 40 months of *Nightline* because it's considered the best and most influential TV news program. What we analyzed was who got on the air and who didn't get on the air as experts to discuss foreign and domestic policy. What we found is that *Nightline* tilted toward the conservative white male establishment. The four guests who appeared most frequently on *Nightline* were Henry Kissinger, Alexander Haig, Jerry Falwell and Elliott Abrams, all supporters of Reaganite policies through that decade. What we found is that critics of U.S. policy rarely appeared on *Nightline*. Whites appeared 90 percent of the time; men appeared 90 percent of the time. So, in a society that the media always tells us is a great, pluralistic society, what you found when you watched *Nightline's* experts is that they reflected a very narrow, conservative elite. We did certain case studies. We studied all of the programs that *Nightline* did on Central America. We found that, of the 68 experts that were allowed onto *Nightline* in a 40-month period, only two of them represented groups critical of Central America policy. We studied all of the programs that *Nightline* did on U.S.-Soviet relations or the Soviet Union, and we found that 50 percent of the guests, half of the guest experts, were former or current U.S. government officials. Less than 1 percent of the guests were representatives of peace orga-

nizations. So you had a ratio of 50 to 1. We also studied
the kinds of foci that *Nightline* had in framing the programs. Obviously, they chose guests after they decided
that the frame would be a certain way and they were going
to look at certain countries in a certain way. We took note
of the fact that throughout its term in office, the Reagan
administration had a media strategy. That was to try to
focus mass media attention on every real or imagined
peccadillo in Nicaragua while simultaneously shifting
attention away from the far worse human rights offenders
in Guatemala or El Salvador, or even Honduras. What we
found was a little bit horrifying. Knowing what the
Reagan administration's media strategy was, we then
looked at *Nightline's* coverage and we found that they did
about 25 to 27 programs that focused exclusively on problems or conflicts in Nicaragua. Then we looked at how
many programs they did focusing exclusively on El Salvador or Guatemala or Honduras. They didn't do a single
program on any of those countries. So the ability of the
White House to set *Nightline's* agenda in foreign policy
was really awesome. One of the things that we've always
criticized *Nightline* and most of the mainstream media for
is for forgetting that in the United States we're supposed
to have something called separation of press and state.
What we found in looking at *Nightline* is that they were
virtually a propaganda organ for the state. They admitted
it after our findings came out. The findings were explosive.
When we handed them to the TV critics we got major
coverage. This was the first week in February. It was one
of the best publicized studies of news media ever done, and
the TV critics have always been receptive to FAIR's arguments because they have to watch all these news shows,
too, and they see the same experts over and over, and
they're bored by them. We gave them ammunition. The
coverage was very fair to our study. *Nightline* was getting
pilloried by questions and requests for an explanation of
why their guest list was so narrow. They responded by

saying, "Look, the conservatives have been in power.
That's the reason they so dominate our guest list." Our
reaction was instant. Our reaction was, "That's what a
Soviet TV news programmer could have said, pre-
glasnost: Look, these conservative white guys are running
the Kremlin, that's why we put them on TV every night."
When we responded that way, it was quite embarrassing
for *Nightline,* and frankly, I think we won the debate, even
in the mainstream media which, prior to our study and a
little bit afterwards, has always treated Ted Koppel as
somewhat of a demigod. The reason is that TV critics want
serious news coverage, and Ted Koppel provides the one
30-minute focus on a single issue each day. Prior to our
study, he had been really worshipped as at least some
alternative to the ten-second news bite on Guatemala on
our way to five seconds on Sri Lanka. That's what happens
on the 6:30 national news. So we really chipped away at
a god, and what happened in the ensuing weeks is that all
of a sudden *Nightline* started putting on a lot of black
people. The problem is that they weren't getting black
experts to talk about national or international issues.
What we found is that they immediately had a program
on tap dancing. They had a program on blues music. They
had a program on black athletes. We began to wonder if
they were doing a snow job on us, cosmetically. While we
think that those issues are important, the thrust of our
criticism of *Nightline* is that black people and Latinos and
policy critics and progressives and women should be on
television night after night discussing not just blues music
and tap dancing, but economics, domestic policy, foreign
policy. That just hasn't happened on *Nightline,* and our
study, unfortunately, hasn't been able to shift *Nightline*
to change its orientation totally.

   DB: How about *MacNeil-Lehrer* on PBS? That's
often viewed by many people as a classic example of this

centrist type of objective reporting. Can you make any analogies between *Nightline* and *MacNeil-Lehrer?*

We're currently doing a systematic study of *MacNeil-Lehrer,* and our initial findings are that in many ways, it's worse. This is the program that is on supposedly public television, which is a fallacy in this country, that we have something called "public TV." But what we've noticed at *MacNeil-Lehrer* is that, while they have a full hour to spend on the daily news, their list of experts is even more narrow than *Nightline.* They go to the government more frequently than *Nightline,* which is not easy to do. It's not easy to outdo *Nightline* on even more government spokespersons than they have. We've found historically that conservative groups have really liked *MacNeil-Lehrer.* In fact, a couple of years ago at the National Conservative Political Action convention, they took a poll of the conservative activists in attendance and they voted *MacNeil-Lehrer* to be "the most balanced network news show." We have a quote of Lehrer where staff members were proposing—this was years ago—that certain public interest leaders or progressive policy critics get on TV, and his reaction was, "Oh, come on, don't give me another one of these moaners or whiners." That was Jim Lehrer's attitude toward people who criticize policy. Recently, some people who are obviously reading *Extra* out in Berkeley attended an event where MacNeil was doing a book-signing party at Cody's Books and, as it's been reported to me, they really peppered MacNeil with questions: "How come you never have representatives of the American left discussing things on your program?" And MacNeil is alleged to have said something like, "There is no American left." So it's obvious when you look at *MacNeil-Lehrer,* they typically have had debates throughout the 1980s on such topics as the nuclear arms race, where the hawkish pole would be represented by someone like Richard Perle or Casper Weinberger, and debating for the dove side would often be Senator Sam Nunn from Georgia, who according to SANE had a 25 percent voting record as a "peace senator." So they set up this narrow debate, where it's someone from the far right debating someone from the near right on foreign policy. On issues of Iran/Contra and covert operations in Central America, typically the person representing the dove pole, the critics' pole, was Senator Boren from Oklahoma. Again, he's somewhat on the near right on those issues, and he'd be debating someone further to his right. So what you find when you look at *Nightline* and *MacNeil-Lehrer* is that generally half of the political spectrum is excluded from debate, and that plays a very important opinion-shaping role for the mainstream journalists. Many print journalists swear by *Nightline*. They watch *Nightline* and then go to sleep and the next day they write their stories. I really feel that *Nightline* and *MacNeil-Lehrer* play an important role in defining what is legitimate opposition and what isn't, and unfortunately, on foreign policy issues, legitimate opposition for *Nightline* and *MacNeil-Lehrer* seems to stop at Senators Nunn and Boren.

DB: To continue with PBS, WNYC, the public TV station in New York, was distributing a weekly investigative news program called the *Kwitny Report*. What happened to that program?

The *Kwitny Report* probed issues like the Guatemalan death squads, and they scored a first in American television when they probed who was killing the workers trying to organize unions or the peasants organizing unions in Guatemala. What they found is that the people behind the killings were often U.S. companies like Coca-Cola and United Brand. What Jonathan Kwitny once reported in a two-part special on Guatemalan death squads is that, as they were giving incidences of murders of union activists, they put up the logos of the U.S. corporations, so you'd hear Jonathan Kwitny talking about the killings of unionists and then you'd see Coca-Cola's logo up on the screen on American television. The breakthrough there is that, historically, the only time you see a corporate logo on American TV is usually when it's been preceded by a smiling woman model telling you that Coca-Cola will make your life more sexy. Here was an investigative reporter with a hard-hitting, well-documented report telling you that behind these corporate logos there's a lot of murder and death in Central America. Obviously that kind of program made bureaucrats at PBS and at this particular station, WNYC, a little bit nervous, and Jonathan Kwitny reports that the new vice president for television at that particular station was often interfering with the copy, the actual product that he was trying to put on the air. He had been given some assurances that he'd have some journalistic freedom, but there was a lot of meddling going on, and then his show was terminated. The official reason was "lack of funding." There is a lot of truth to that factor as well. A program like the *Kwitny Report* has trouble getting funding from the typical people who fund public broadcasting. Those people are the major oil companies, the electrical companies. The underwriter of *MacNeil-Lehrer,* the main underwriter, is AT&T, a military contractor, which may explain why Sam Nunn is usually the most left-wing speaker on the arms race on *MacNeil-Lehrer.* So Jonathan Kwitny was really in a bind, and it's the typical bind that you have at public broadcasting. They really aren't a public network. The corporations have made many inroads into public television, perhaps more so, than they have on the commercial networks, and I'll tell you why. Let me give you an anecdote which I think symbolizes what's wrong with American television in general and public television in particular.

Ten or twelve years ago, there was a fringe right-wing columnist named John McLaughlin. In 1990, he's one of the main players in American political discourse.

He's one of the biggest faces on American television. What happened was, about ten years ago some businesses got behind McLaughlin. The United States was just coming out of the oil crisis of the mid-1970s. Some big businesses said, "We aren't going to put our money just behind ballets and high-brow culture on public TV any more. We're going to put our money behind conservative propagandists who have a pro-corporate view." It was conscious at Mobil Oil. It was conscious at several other corporations that had been influenced by a right-wing group called Accuracy in Media, a misnamed group. McLaughlin was one of the beneficiaries of this new corporate strategy. A couple corporations got behind him, most particularly the Edison Institute, which is the electrical industry lobby. The Edison Institute put together a program hosted by McLaughlin, who had been with the conservative magazine *National Review*. This McLaughlin group was a center right group. It was given for free to any public TV channel which would take it, because the electrical industry was underwriting it. What happened was, a lot of public TV stations don't have a lot of money, and what this program did was to almost wipe off the map a more middle-of-the-road show called *Agronsky and Company*. It began to take off. When it took off, General Electric became its underwriter. On the strength of McLaughlin's show appearing on PBS on hundreds of stations, they started a new program for McLaughlin called *One on One* where he interviews a newsmaker from his conservative frame of reference. This one was sponsored by Pepsi-Cola and Metropolitan Life. Then, while those two programs were taking off, General Electric, in the intervening years, purchased NBC, the biggest television network in the country. Then they set up a cable network called CNBC. Every night now in prime time, at 10:00, John McLaughlin has the *John McLaughlin Show*. So you have an individual who ten or twelve years ago was a fringe right-wing columnist and today is one of the biggest faces in American political television. That's purely because of the power that the corporations have: "You know, I like this McLaughlin. I'm going to give him yet a second show. And a third show." And, of course, the same corporations which ultimately are deciding who hosts a TV show and who doesn't are deciding by default that, "Well, I'm not going to give any money to Jonathan Kwitny. He just put my corporate logo up on his TV program saying that I'm killing nuns and priests and union organizers in Guatemala." So it's obvious, the problem that we have in terms of TV censorship. TV censorship in American society done, of course, by corporations. It isn't done by religious fanatics or by the government. Corporations are the main censors in U.S. society. Obviously, because of that, the media are so controlled by big corporations that they don't define such censorship as censorship.

DB: What are your views on National Public Radio?

NPR, years ago, used to provide somewhat of an alternative in their longer-running features, their ability to go more in depth. But what's happened in the last few years is a very disturbing process where their product has become more and more mainstream. You see virtually the same experts on television, the same conservative, narrow experts, from center to right, appearing on NPR. You have them mainstreaming so badly that sometimes they just cover foreign countries by asking the *New York Times* reporter who's stationed in that country to talk about it. God forbid; the *New York Times* has enough power in the media in setting the agenda for American television networks and their nightly and morning news shows. If NPR really wanted to provide an alternative, the last thing they would do is just to serve up more *New York Times* correspondents. So it's a disturbing process, but I'm optimistic in one sense. In some cities NPR is, unfortunately, the only alternative. Many cities don't have Pacifica Radio, which is a true alternative. So what's happened lately, especially since FAIR was born in 1986, is that we're telling these NPR fanatics to quit complaining to FAIR and start taking their complaints directly to the NPR stations and directly to *All Things Considered, Morning Edition,* and *Weekend Edition.* That's happening more and more. I think the NPR journalists are generally tougher, better than the typical mainstream reporter. If they hear from an aroused public, it's possible that NPR could get back on track and be more of an alternative, which is how it started out many years ago.

DB: One of the NPR commentators is Daniel Schorr. He had an op-ed piece in the *New York Times* in November of 1989. You talk about that in one of your *Extra* issues. It's an interesting little thing. It's a commentary he did on the radio as well.

Right. Daniel Schorr is unfortunately a cold warrior when it comes to foreign policy. He's in no way an alternative voice on foreign policy. In fact, he picked up an Associated Press canard that had obviously been planted by U.S. intelligence. We traced this AP lie to its bureau in Tokyo. It was this lie that Nicaragua had endorsed the Chinese crackdown on the students in Tiananmen Square. Daniel Schorr took this lie weeks after it had already been retracted by Associated Press because of the work FAIR, Alexander Cockburn and other media critics had done to prove that it was a lie. He took this hoax that the Nicaraguan government supported the Chinese crackdown and put it on a commentary on NPR, which was picked up as an op-ed piece in the *New York Times.* What was interesting is that, because a lot of NPR listeners are part of the FAIR media activist network, they knew instantly when they saw it in the *New York Times* and heard it on NPR, "My God, Daniel Schorr has dredged up this hoax that's already been retracted by Associated Press."

They deluged NPR with angry letters and calls. Pretty soon NPR apologized and Daniel Schorr was sending out a form letter to NPR listeners saying, "I'm sorry I got it wrong. I didn't know it had been retracted." The *New York Times* never retracted it at all, and I think that's a mark of what I'm getting at here. That as mainstream as NPR executives want it to become, there are many journalists at NPR, and most of its listeners, that don't want it to be just another *New York Times* over the air. There is this militant listenership that, if mobilized, could exert some rectifying influence on NPR. On the other hand, the *New York Times* just ignored the fact that they had gotten it wrong. We can review the *New York Times* in detail, because we have a track record of showing their hoaxes and getting retractions. What we've noticed is that a lot of times when we prove the *New York Times* wrong we'll get a letter back from someone at the *Times* saying, "Yeah, you're right, but that's not my department. Complain to the op-ed editor." That's just exactly what happens with us, so the *New York Times* didn't bother retracting that one, although they retracted about ten other lies about Central America that we've caught them on.

Examples

The Five O'Clock Follies

Then and Now

Mark Hertsgaard

March 15, 1991

DB: In your book, *On Bended Knee,* you cite Reagan Deputy Chief of Staff Michael Deaver as saying that he knew all along that the press would submit to censorship of the Grenada operation without too great a fuss. What was the source of Deaver's confidence?

Deaver had enormous confidence in his own abilities, but I think he also had a very clear-eyed appreciation that the media, at least, believed that they needed the White House more than vice versa. In fact, that was a questionable assumption. Any time that the White House correspondents of the three major networks wanted to make trouble for Ronald Reagan, they usually could. But most of the time they refrained. In the Grenada example, what Deaver saw that, as he put it: "This was going to be a very positive story. As a result, it was very unlikely that the media were going to take us on." At that point the American public "was so hungry for a victory that if we had found an island someplace with two natives on it, stuck our flag on it and said, by God, it's ours, they would have supported the idea." However, it's important to note in Grenada that Deaver was very, very worried about preventing pictures being taken of the reality of warfare on the ground. He did realize that the American public, as we've seen again in the Gulf War, needed to have a sanitized portrayal of warfare. If they were forced to come face to face with the realities of war, that is, that soldiers get their guts blown out and that civilians have their heads blown off and entire villages are destroyed, then public opinion would have turned around in a hurry. That's why Deaver very strongly supported the decision to keep the press out.

DB: You write, Reagan officials had "a campaign to transform journalists from independent professionals into obedient functionaries of the national security bureaucracy." I'd like you to look at your assumption there about "independent professionals." The assumption is that the journalists covering the White House beat are indeed independent and they were transformed during the Reagan era.

I think that, at least in theory, they are supposed to be independent. The whole idea of the First Amendment in this country and the ideal of a free and independent press standing as a check and balance against the government is that these journalists are going to stand apart, that they will, in effect, stand in for the average citizen. The average citizen doesn't have the time or resources to acquire all the information necessary to make the kinds of choices required of a citizen in a democracy. You can't go and hear the press secretary speak. You can't attend the congressional hearings. You can't weigh all the options. That's why we have reporters and a press. In that sense, it's entirely accurate to say that these journalists were supposed to be independent. The reality of the Washington press corps, as I write in *On Bended Knee,* is that, for the most part, they're a palace court press. They are *not* terribly independent. In fact, they are highly dependent mainly on their sources within Washington officialdom. What the Reagan people did was to intensify the existing situation, in which the press at best criticizes the president around the margins and very rarely stands apart and offers truly alternative perspectives on what is coming out of the White House.

DB: What role did Vice President Bush play in the Reagan effort to control and manipulate the media?

So far as I know, very little. Bush was not a player in that regard. The White House PR apparatus during the Reagan years was by and large a creature run by Jim Baker, who was then White House Chief of Staff, now Secretary of State. Mike Deaver, Dave Gergen, who had worked in the Nixon and Ford White House and went on to become a commentator for *MacNeil-Lehrer*, and Dick Darman, who's now the Director of the Budget for President Bush, were all critical to it. Certainly, Gergen, Darman and Baker all came out of the Bush wing of the Republican party. All three of them, I believe, certainly Baker and Gergen, were very actively involved with Bush's 1980 presidential campaign. *He* was their candidate in 1980, not Ronald Reagan. I think that was true of Darman as well. In that sense, certainly what they did was far from anathema to George Bush, but I don't think Bush had any hands-on role.

DB: Talk, if you will, about the first Bush war, the invasion of Panama in December 1989. How was the press coverage of that?

In that case, I think that it was essentially Grenada II, if you will. The PR, as far as I could determine, was run mainly out of the Pentagon, again as it was in Grenada. There was obviously collaboration with the White House press office in Grenada, but the operative decisions were being made in the Pentagon and the White House was then executing them. For example, with Panama, it was the Pentagon which decided to keep the press from coming to cover the invasion. When the media finally did pull together a pool of reporters and get them down there, they were basically kept incommunicado for the early hours of the fighting, and after that were not let out to see anything really important for quite a while. Again, that was just an extension of what the government had learned in Grenada.

I must say, on the other side, that the press didn't respond any better than it did during Grenada. Once again, they were very understanding about the military's desire for censorship. They did not resist it very strongly. Even when the censorship was relaxed somewhat and there came to be more reporters down there, very few paid any attention to stories other than those the Pentagon wanted covered. The basic thrust of the Panama coverage was "getting Noriega." Are we going to get him or aren't we? As a result of some ineffectiveness on the part of the U.S. military, the Panama invasion story got some negative play for a few days because, if you remember, they couldn't find Noriega. But it was all within the context of "Noriega is the bad guy." Once again another parallel to Grenada. The entire story was framed within a "good guys/bad guys" context, very much along the lines of what the Pentagon wanted. The only criticisms that you heard from the press were essentially logistical criticisms: how well are they carrying out this goal of getting Noriega? The fact that the U.S. military destroyed an entire neighborhood, El Chorrillo, in the process of doing that got very little attention. Very few reporters cared very much about civilian casualties. You and I were just sitting here watching Fred Francis on the NBC Nightly News. It happens that Fred Francis was the TV reporter in that pool. Afterwards, I was doing a story on the Panama coverage for Rolling Stone, and I asked Francis why there wasn't more coverage of the civilian casualties. He said, "Look, I'm a military correspondent, and this was a war. In a war involving 25,000 American troops, the fact that there are 300 or 400 civilian casualties to me does not constitute a major story."

When you have a so-called independent journalist who has that as a working assumption, you don't have to work very hard if you're the government propagandist to make sure that he reports the kind of stories you want to see.

DB: If, in fact, the press is so servile and obedient, why is the government creating this elaborate apparatus to control it?

The press is nowhere near as servile and obedient as a lot of left-wing critics like to say. A lot of times the Left does not give credit where credit is due to reporters. They have a very monolithic view of the press. They think because they don't see their own views represented on the front page every day, that it's the press's fault and it's all a case of "because GE owns NBC we're never going to see anything critical about the military budget on NBC." I think, frankly, that that's the worst kind of infantile, anti-intellectual leftism. To use a phrase that's no longer so fashionable, you have to take a more dialectical approach than that. There are many reporters who do believe in the traditional adversarial role of the press and who try very hard to report what's going on. That's one part of it, that it's not quite as black and white as a lot of people on the Left think.

Secondly, while it's very true that the Washington press corps is essentially a palace court press, nevertheless they end up reporting a lot of information that the people in the palace don't like. What are they reporting on? Essentially, on the different factions within the palace. So if you're a Republican president, like Ronald Reagan, and you come up with an idea like SDI, the Strategic Defense Initiative, one of the very few ideas that really did excite genuine dissent within the Washington establishment during the 1980s, and the press talks to people like Robert McNamara, former Secretary of Defense, or Sam Nunn, the Senate Democrat who has a very strong record on military matters, and they're criticizing SDI, that's going to create problems for you if you're the White House press secretary. They're going to be releasing information and stories that will be on the front page, saying that SDI doesn't work. So there are differences within the ruling class, if you will, and the press will always play on that. Finally, there is the fact, to quote my dear old friend, the late I.F. Stone, that the government puts out so much information that it can't help but let the truth slip out from time to time. And the press is going to report that. If you're the president, that can often cause trouble, too.

DB: Where does the war in Indochina fit into this construct of Panama, Grenada, the coverage of the contra war in the 1980s and the Gulf War in the 1990s?

Vietnam remains the foundation of a lot of the ideological content within the news media community, and of the ideological struggles that are still carrying on. One of the important things about the Gulf coverage was, in a way, that there was an attempt to make amends for Vietnam, on both sides, the military and the press. George Bush kept saying that "we're not going to fight this war like Vietnam, we're not going to fight with one hand tied behind our back," which of course is a blasphemy against history, the idea that somehow the United States fought in Vietnam with a hand tied behind its back. But be that as it may, the generals in the Pentagon were equally determined that this war was not going to be covered the way Vietnam was. By no means is the common critique— that the press lost the Vietnam War— accurate. However, the press at that time *did* begin to reflect some of the schisms within the political class in this country, some of the divisions within the ruling elite.

Increasingly, as the 1960s wore on into the 1970s and the war was going nowhere, you began to see more and more criticism coming out. Especially as more and more young men came home in body bags. That did, undeniably, have an effect on public opinion in the country and made it more difficult for the war to be prosecuted. I don't think there's any sense in denying that. As a result, both in Grenada and in Panama and then again in the Gulf, and as you were mentioning, in Central America, there was much more of an emphasis on the part of military propagandists to control what the American public knows. One of the main lessons that the military learned, apropos Central America, is that it's best not to have very many American casualties. If at all possible, hire some other "wogs," to use the British phrase, to do your fighting and dying for you. In that case, the American public won't care. Or, in Grenada and in Panama, you go in with such immense force against such a tiny enemy that you win decisively, and again, they did that in the Gulf. I think that's the major backdrop to all of this. It has gone back to Vietnam the whole time. Again, so much of the right-wing backlash against the press that was coming to a crescendo as Reagan came to power was a response to Vietnam and to Watergate, that somehow the press has become a real threat to the status quo in this country. It helped to overthrow a president.

But again, the misreading of history is appalling. The idea that the press as a whole somehow prosecuted Watergate is simply inaccurate. The fact of it is that the *Washington Post* was alone on that story for months and indeed was battling not just White House propagandists, who were knocking down every story they did, but battling their colleagues and the rest of the press, who were saying that the *Post* was off on a wild goose chase, biased against Nixon. Even people in the *Washington Post's* own newsroom, I think Ben Bagdikian told you about this, since he was right in the middle of all of this stuff, a lot of the old ones were saying that these young Turks Woodward and Bernstein don't know what they're talking about, they should get off the story. It really turned my stomach when

I heard journalists later talk about how gloriously valiant they were with Watergate and Vietnam. That's not at all the case. It plays into the right-wing counterattack that, by the early 1980s, had the press pulling in its horns. In the name of "not being liberal" they stopped being journalists.

DB: Ben Bagdikian also talks about the "designated bad guy." We saw Khomeini, Ortega, Qaddafi, Noriega, Hussein. What role do the media play in terms of this orchestrated campaign to defame and discredit often former allies?

One great failing of the media in this regard is that they're too close to their Washington sources, that for all intents and purposes, most members of the Washington press corps might as well be on the government payroll. They are popularizing whatever the government line of the moment is. So, when Noriega is seen as the bad guy, 95 percent of the coverage repeats that. Then there is the 5 percent coverage of the independent-minded journalists and the lone reporter here and there who say, "Wait, wait, by the way, we were paying him $200,000 a year from the CIA all these years."

Likewise, in the case of Saddam, you did get these dribbles of stories like, "Wait, wait, we've been giving him money all this time and encouraging him and we sided with him against Iran and when Ambassador Glaspie was in that meeting with him, didn't she say that we didn't care how he resolved his border disputes?" But, as Izzie Stone once said, it's not as though those alternative stories never run. They do. But they're on the front page one day and then they're gone. The official line bullshit, as he put it, gets regurgitated day after day, and that takes over in the public mind.

This raises an interesting point, one of the key insights that Deaver had about how you control public consciousness. I don't think he was even specifically aware of it, but it came from his own advertising mentality, which is a very intelligent and acute realization about the way information functions in a modern society. If you're going to have a real impact on how the public thinks, repetition is essential. In an information saturated society, the only thing that pierces the static is the information that gets repeated day after day after day. It doesn't matter how bad a story breaks on Monday. If it is not repeated and doesn't become part of the news cycle, there are going to be other kinds of stories that come on Tuesday, Wednesday, Thursday; by Friday the public is no longer aware of it. Most of them never heard it the first time. Most people have jobs, families, all other kinds of responsibilities. They might have missed the news that day, maybe they were washing the baby at that point in the newscast and didn't quite hear it, and boom! the next day it's gone. What Deaver understood was that every day you have to keep putting out a different variation on the story.

The first eighteen months of Reagan's presidency, Deaver said we are not going to push anything but the economy and economic reform. The reason is that it's going to take that long for us to get control of the public agenda and keep it there. So he would overrule all other kinds of initiatives from elsewhere in the government. Everybody in the government wants the president to speak out for their policy. If they're in education, foreign aid, transportation, they're all pushing the White House to please have the president come speak for this. Deaver cut everyone off at the knees and said, we're going to talk about the economy only. As a result, they got very good penetration of their message. They understood the way that information works in this society.

In that regard, to swing back to your question, it is absolutely essential that the media be complicit. They don't necessarily even have to be conscious of it. But as long as they keep coming in there every day and they're happy to take those pictures and put on the story that Deaver wants, even if they snipe a little bit around the margins, the White House doesn't care. Essentially they've gotten out the story that they want.

DB: Where is that crusading journalist at a presidential press conference, who may be totally opportunistic and cynical and not believe what's he's going to ask the president, standing up and saying, "OK, you're against naked aggression when Iraq invades Kuwait. What about the U.S. invasion of Panama?"

Where is that journalist? If such a journalist existed, it would be very hard for him or her to ask that question. Anyone to whom such a question would occur, it would probably be evident in their reporting long before that. As a result, it would be very unlikely that he or she would be invited to such a briefing in the first place and almost inconceivable that he or she actually would be called upon. Somebody like Sam Donaldson of ABC or Helen Thomas of UPI always gets a chance to ask their questions. Occasionally, they would ask at least an apparently, and sometimes a genuinely sharp-edged question. My beef then is that nobody else in the press follows up. Any politician worth his salt is going to be able to dodge a question once. But when you're on live television it becomes quickly apparent if you dodge it twice or three times. The problem is that the reporters don't follow up each other's questions.

So when Helen Thomas asks, in May of 1982, as she did, "Why are you opposed to a freeze of nuclear weapons?" and Reagan says something to the effect of, "Well, you know, the Soviets are ahead of us in nuclear armaments production," somebody else needs then to stand up and say, "Mr. President, wait. Nobody else in the government believes that. What's your source of information?" When Reagan stands up and says, "You can always call back a nuclear missile once you've shot it," somebody needs to stand up and say, "Mr. President, did you misspeak yourself when you said that?"

But that doesn't happen. It's because the crusading journalist is really not what the system produces. It doesn't produce that within the news organizations, and if it does, that journalist finds it very difficult to operate within the government. The press secretary does not return your calls. He does not respond to your requests for information. You've got to be able to do the routine stuff as well as the crusading stuff. So I think it's almost impossible to expect that kind of journalism on a consistent basis.

DB: Erwin Knoll, the editor of *The Progressive*, tells the story of how, when he was the White House correspondent for The Newhouse Newspapers in the mid-1960s, he did indeed have the temerity to ask Lyndon Johnson some questions on his policy in Indochina. That was the end of his career, essentially, as a Washington correspondent. So that goes again to the whole process of socialization that is at work here, a cultural process. What are the perks, not to mention the high salaries, that these journalists receive?

Let's mention the high salaries that these journalists receive. One of the things that Mike Deaver said is, look, we knew that they were going to take the stories we wanted because these White House correspondents are getting paid very handsome six-figure salaries. Their networks are not going to keep paying them that if they don't get pictures of the president on every night. Those men and women want to be on the tube every night. If that means that essentially you've got to do the story Mike Deaver's laid out for you, OK. You'll do your best to get a balancing sound bite from a Democratic politician, but in essence you're going to be talking about what the White

House wants you to talk about. That's part of it. Also, just
the proximity to power. You're just too close to power, and
you're in that Washington world where everybody goes to
the same dinner parties and cocktail parties and tries to
trade access. Brit Hume, who is now the White House
correspondent for *ABC News*, was a reporter who started
with Jack Anderson and did some real investigative work
many years ago. Now he plays tennis with the President.
That's too close.

DB: Let's talk about media coverage of the Gulf War.
You called it "a 1990s version of the 5 o'clock follies." What
do you mean by that?

The 5 o'clock follies were this exercise in propaganda
that occurred during Vietnam when, at 5 o'clock every
afternoon, the U.S. military briefers would get the reporters together and feed them a lot of generally inflated
information on what was going on in the field. They were
called the 5 o'clock follies because, at a certain point,
reporters just began to laugh at what they were being told.
The reason I said that about the Gulf War is that is seems
to me that much the same thing was happening. You
would see these reporters standing up, and they all had
the same backdrops. They were all on the top of the same
hotel in Riyad and there they were, with their flak jackets
and safari jackets, trying to look the part of the dashing
foreign correspondent and giving us all this information,
but not having the candor to admit that, essentially, it was
all government and military supplied information. For all
we knew, the military briefer was standing 20 feet off
camera. So that's why I say that it was very much like the
5 o'clock follies. We got essentially the military's version
of this war.

DB: Do you think, given Grenada and Panama and
now the Gulf War, that we've seen the last of the living

room wars, which Vietnam represented, to use Michael
Arlen's term?

Have we seen the last of the living room wars? I'm
not sure that I would agree with that. In fact, this was a
living room war, but a sanitized war.

DB: You didn't see Morley Safer in a village at Cam
Ne, as he was in 1965, showing Marines torching a village.

No, but this was still very definitely a living room
war, except it was made into a great TV mini-series
instead of a living room war that was disconcerting to the
viewers. In a way, what they learned from Vietnam was,
OK, if we're going to have a living room war, let's have it
be a war where we're the good guys, there's no blood, and
we win really easy. That's what they did. They kept the
American public from the horror and carnage that are the
reality of modern warfare. They kept everything very
clean, very abstract and quite bloodless. They talked
about "2,000 sorties a day." They used all of the military
terminology. That's why I say it was a very military view
of the war. I saw so many of these stories that had the sort
of "gee whiz" aspect, like "Well look at this, we can actually
refuel our planes on the way to combat. Look at this
wonderful tank and how that works." I'm sure in the mind
of the military PR guys that it was very wholesome stuff.

But it had almost nothing to do with what was really
going on there, which was essentially a massacre. The
American journalists never used words like "massacre" to
describe what was going on. They never used words like
"carpet bombing," another Vietnam term. If they had, I
think there would have been more of a possibility that the
American public would have had to come face to face with
what their tax dollars were doing in Kuwait and Iraq.
Instead, once again, it was framed as a good guys/bad guys

morality play in the context of stopping Saddam and his aggression.

One of the other problems with the press is that they bring virtually zero historical perspective to these conflicts. With the combination of that and how close they are to American government policy, the American public had no sense of the hypocrisy of the official American position here, no sense of the utter double standard that American policy represents in the Middle East. Therefore, the American public had no understanding of why the Arab world distrusts America and why they may, at some points, have been supportive of Saddam. You never heard a full and candid explanation of how the United States stands behind Israel. One of the great things about the Gulf coverage, the happiest reporters out of the Gulf coverage had to be the U.N. reporters, because suddenly their superiors discovered the U.N. again. In Panama, you may remember, the U.N. voted 85 to 20 to condemn the invasion as a flagrant violation of international law. On December 29, 1989, I turned on my evening news. NBC: no mention. CBS found time to lavish a full ten seconds on that story.

You compare that with how much we heard about the U.N. and Iraq and Kuwait, and suddenly the U.N. has been transformed from this non-existent backwater at the time of Panama or, God knows, the war on Nicaragua into the most august and morally upstanding body in the world. That is an example of the press following the ideological lead of the American government and leading to a rather distorted impression of what was really going on there.

You want to talk about U.N. resolutions, let's not just talk about Kuwait. Let's talk about Cyprus. Let's talk about how for sixteen years the U.N. has said that Turkey—an American ally, a NATO ally, very important in the coalition against Iraq—Turkey was supposed to pull out of Cyprus sixteen years ago. Israel was supposed to pull out of the occupied territories 23 years ago. Or, if

we're against aggression, what about what China did to
Tibet just months before what happened in Iraq? The
American media simply do not bring up these kinds of
countervailing perspectives. Supposedly to do that would
be ideological, editorializing. They say, "we can't do that.
We're supposed to be down the middle. The only way we
can report that is if the opposition party says that." I think
that's the worst cop-out there is. People around the world
have died and would be willing to die to have the kind of
freedoms that we take for granted in this country, and for
the press to not live up to its responsibilities in that regard
is nothing short of shameful.

DB: At that same time, December 1989 and January
1990, the Security Council in fact passed resolutions con-
demning the U.S. invasion of Panama. Those resolutions
were vetoed by the United States.

Yes. Those resolutions were vetoed. To bring it up to
date with the Gulf War, in December of 1990 the U.N.
General Assembly passed by a vote of 144 to 2, a resolution
calling for a conference on peace in the Middle East,
which, as you know, was one of the main sticking points
between Iraq and the United States prior to the war. I
needn't tell you which two countries voted against it. That
vote was reported in about the tenth paragraph of a story
on about page 11 of the *New York Times.* That kind of
news judgment, again, is a very clear reflection of the
manner in which even a great newspaper—which I think
the *New York Times,* with all of its flaws, is—even the best
newspaper in this country still follows the government
line.

DB: How did the *Times* cover Security Council and
General Assembly votes on the Soviet invasion of Afghanistan? Was that relegated to the back pages?

No, of course not. They ended up carrying an ideological banner. At the same time, it is somewhat complicated. When the World Court voted to condemn the Reagan administration war on Nicaragua as a violation of international law, all three network evening newscasts led with that story. It was a front-page story in the *Washington Post* and the *New York Times*. It's not always black and white. Your Afghanistan question is a good one because it shows how, on the other side, those stories get played up very big all the time. Here it's much less of a sure thing that we're going to go against our own government. In some ways that's more important if you're a journalist. We live in this country. This is the government that we can affect, the polity to which we have real responsibility, and this is where you have an obligation to stand up for truth, especially when it's uncomfortable.

DB: Edward Said has called the question of Palestine "very inconvenient" for U.S. journalists. It's not a topic or subject that most journalists gravitate to, and if they do, it's often couched in terms of terrorism and that kind of imagery.

Yes. The reason that Palestine and Palestinians are an inconvenient subject is that Israel is such a difficult subject. Israel is the major U.S. client in the region, the locus of the double standard that the United States has followed there for so long, and it's always difficult when you are a Washington reporter to stand up and say, "Naked, not so! That's not the way it is!" or to call a spade a spade, especially in regard to Israel, which is a client in what is probably the most important geostrategic area in the world because of all the oil there. And yet, if you look at it on so-called moral grounds, it's very hard to argue against that. If we're going to be talking about U.N. resolutions on Kuwait, how can you avoid the U.N. resolutions regarding Palestine?

DB: Again, to cite something that Ben Bagdikian talks about, the "zones of silence," literally areas where journalists never tread—not fear to tread, but just don't enter—specific areas of examining the structural relations of power and privilege in this country.

No, they don't talk about that.

DB: Why not?

Because it pretty quickly becomes communicated to you that that's not what your editors and your producers want to hear. That is seen as—and I've heard a lot of them in regard to my own reporting—"that's predictable," "you're whining," "you have an ideological bent." Why is that? I think it's very clear. It has to do with the role that the news organizations play in this society. They are central pillars of the establishment. For the most part they are owned by very wealthy people or wealthy corporations who have an abiding interest in the status quo. Nobody who has an abiding interest in the status quo is going to want to pay reporters to go out and challenge that. There are countervailing factors to that in much the same way as there are with a democracy.

Let's take the Democratic Party. The Democratic Party always has a contradiction between its mass base and its elite funders. The elite funders basically want to move the party to the right, but if the party is going to win any elections it has to placate the mass base. You can look at a newspaper publisher and editor in much the same way. An editor has to serve his publisher, who is generally a conservative person. At the same time, he has to be selling newspapers. If most of the people in his community are out of work or can't find adequate health care, to some extent if he's going to be selling newspapers he has to have some reflection of the social reality out there. It's a very difficult tightrope. So you'll have reporters who occasionally do stories that step beyond the envelope, but for the most part, the overwhelming majority of coverage is going to be coverage that supports the status quo.

DB: Do you think most journalists are aware of what is called the "political economy of the mass media"?

No, of course not. Most journalists are mainly worried about getting ahead. That means getting the stories in on time and fighting with their editors. They are aware of the political economy of the mass media in a visceral sense. They're usually not very conscious of it, but they're swimming in it every day. But their consciousness of that usually is not terribly good. Especially with the elite papers and networks where, to some extent, they've been bought off. They are now members of the social elite, the upper-middle class. In Washington in particular, most reporters at the big quality newspapers or the networks are making $60,000 or $70,000 a year. That puts you immediately in the top 10 percent of the population. And yet, I can think back to countless times when those very reporters would be talking about how they're having trouble making enough money. That is going to make it very difficult for you to truly empathize with the average person to do a good job of reporting *their* reality. I'm not saying that just because you make a lot of money you can no longer empathize with the working class. I think Bruce Springsteen is an example of how that's simplistic. But for the most part, if you're making that much money, you don't care very much about the average person. I think you have much more of an ideological predisposition to accept the rather mean-spirited policies of a Ronald Reagan or a George Bush, who at least covers up the mean-spiritedness with the rhetoric of compassion.

DB: In *On Bended Knee*, you mention the cave dwellers, the perennial residents of the Washington establishment. We just talked about some journalists earning $60,000 or $70,000 and not making ends meet. Then you have the millionaires, the Rathers and the Wallaces and the whole elite corps that that represents.

Yes. I'll tell you a good story that I think puts this all into a nutshell. In Ronald Reagan's second term, he came out with what was supposed to be the centerpiece of his domestic program: tax reform. Big promotional effort to sell it in Congress. Dan Rather was doing a special report on it one night on the evening news. Phil Jones, his Capitol Hill correspondent, a good, strong reporter, had gone through explaining what the proposals were.

Then they engaged in "cross-talk," where Dan was interviewing Phil. That's a marketing device. It's supposed to make the viewer at home feel like he's part of the news team. So Rather said to Phil Jones, "Phil, how will these new tax changes affect my pocketbook and the pocketbooks of millions of Americans?" An honest answer on the part of Phil Jones is, "Well, Dan, since you make about $2.5 million a year, you'll get a tax break of some $200,000 this year, while the average American will get 20 bucks, maybe 25." Of course, Phil Jones couldn't say anything like that if he ever wanted to work in network television again.

I tell that story partly because it reveals something about the way that correspondents go back and forth, but also because there is this urge, on the part of anchors especially, to play themselves as the average guy, the American Everyman, and Rather wants to come across as, "I'm just like you all." You're just like all of us except you make $2.5 million a year. It's like that wonderful old line of Hemingway's when Fitzgerald said to him that the rich are different from us, and Hemingway said, yeah, they have a lot more money.

DB: Let's talk about this seeming inability of the media to look at causes of symptoms. For example, the *New York Times* does in fact report that infant mortality rates are increasing in the United States. It's front-page news. It does report that the level of illiteracy in the United States is increasing rather dramatically in the last few years. But there are no connections made as to root causes. It's just offered as raw information, like "the temperature today is 56 degrees and the wind is blowing from the southeast at twelve miles per hour."

I think that's one of the greatest failures of our media and one of the most frustrating. Why that is, I can give you some explanations, but they never quite satisfy me. The explanations are: that's the kind of reporting that raises very serious and pointed questions about the way our society is organized, about power relations in our society, about the advantages of and problems with a capitalist system. It raises real questions about the status quo. Those questions are not going to be asked on a consistent basis within news organizations that are owned by corporations that have every interest in maintaining the status quo. Those corporations are not going to hire individuals to run those organizations who care about that kind of reporting. Therefore, those individuals are not going to hire reporters who do that kind of reporting, and so you're not going to see it. If a reporter somehow does come along and try to do that kind of reporting, he/she will get stopped. He or she gets told, that's not what we want, or, that story doesn't quite work, or, you're too close to that story, or, you have an ideological bent, or, this is getting somewhat predictable. I've heard all of these things, and I know reporters who have heard all of them. Sometimes the most interesting part of that comes from reporters who have not been socialized. Generally, if you start as a reporter early in your career you pick up the messages and it becomes almost instinctive. You don't even realize all of what you've given up, all of the small compromises that you've made along the way.

Ray Bonner, for example, who did some marvelous and very brave reporting for the *New York Times* on El Salvador in 1981 and 1982, really broke a lot of the stories about the military violations of human rights there, the death squads; part of the reason that Bonner did that reporting was that he came to journalism as a second career relatively late in his life. He was in his late thirties. He left a career as a Washington lawyer and just started to do reporting and suddenly found himself stringing for the *New York Times*. He had never been socialized within the *New York Times* structure. He didn't know what was against the rules until it was too late and he eventually lost his job. So when you ask why they don't go for more structural explanations, it's because that sort of thinking is leached out of you long ago in the socialization process within the media. It's very much like what happens in the other areas of the consciousness machine in this society, the universities or the educational system. That kind of critical thinking is not encouraged.

DB: You've certainly covered some of the bleak spots. Talk about some of the bright spots that you would recommend, that you turn to for news and information.

That's a tough one. I'm a little biased because I write for them myself, but I think the *New Yorker* is an excellent source of information. I'm very proud of the coverage that we've done on the Gulf War in the Notes and Comments section of the Talk of the Town. I think we've been quite tough and asked a lot of the right questions. Beyond that, I try to read a wide range of things. There's a lot of stuff in the *New York Times* which I read, but you have to read between the lines. You have to know the ideological bias of the *Times* so you can glean the information from it. Television, for the most part, is worthless, but if you're

going to watch one of the three network evening newscasts, I would watch ABC.

DB: Why?

I think that, for one thing, Jennings is simply a more
worldly anchor and an anchor does have a major imprint
on those shows; partly because he's Canadian he doesn't
have the pro-American bias, and partly because he's spent
a lot of time abroad, he recognizes that it's not as black
and white as most Americans believe. I'm not holding up
ABC as the paragon of virtue here, but of the network
evening newscasts, I would go there. I think that *All
Things Considered* oftentimes does very good coverage.

Occasionally you find some excellent individual reports on the front page of the *Wall Street Journal*. What's
always amazing about it is how it so contradicts what you
see on the editorial pages. Their reporter Susan Faludi
did a story about six months ago, on leveraged buyouts
and how it had worked at Safeway, that was the crispest
and most searing anatomy of the brutal workings of capitalism at its most rapacious and the human costs of it
that you would want to see anywhere. Of course, the
alternative press is very important to me. I read things
like *Greenpeace* magazine. *Extra* is an excellent publication from the Fairness and Accuracy in Reporting group.
I read *The Nation*. I also try, every once in a while, to read
people I disagree with. I think that's always very useful.
And above all—and again I have a bias here because I
write them—but read books. If you really want to know,
read books. You've got to have some kind of historical
perspective. So much of what is problematic about our
news media coverage comes from its insistent focus on
"now, now, now." If something happened two days ago the
media do not care about it. That's a real failing.

DB: I notice in your list that you omitted Nightline and MacNeil-Lehrer. What's your take on those programs?

I do watch *MacNeil-Lehrer* quite a bit, but that's mainly because it's on in the hour between CBS news and ABC. I think that *MacNeil-Lehrer,* every once in a while— and I would say the same for *Nightline*— every once in a while they have something excellent. *MacNeil-Lehrer* occasionally picks up very good reports from British television. They'll do a 20-minute piece on famine in the Horn of Africa. They were on to that long before the networks.

But having said that, I would say that for the most part, *MacNeil-Lehrer* is the worst example of this loony idea of objectivity and balance run amok. You will have two sides to everything. There is one person who says that mass destruction is a terrible thing and another who says the weapons of mass destruction are a wonderful thing. Let's talk about it. As if every issue has to have the two sides. Both of those shows, as the FAIR report says, have an appalling fealty to Washington officialdom. Very Washingtoncentric. It's such a problem. They've gotten a little bit better because of FAIR's tweaking of at *MacNeil-Lehrer.* But for the most part, what you hear on *MacNeil-Lehrer* reinforces something that I wrote during the Gulf coverage, which is that we do not have a government run press in this country, thank God, but we do have a government friendly press. For the most part, the people that you see on *MacNeil-Lehrer* are giving you the government line. Thank you very much, but I can get that from commercial television. I want to see something that's alternative, something a little bit broader. Again, the same thing goes for *Nightline.* Every once in a while there will be something quite excellent, about one night out of five or ten. For the most part it's the same tired faces giving you the same line of bullshit.

Stenographers to Power

The Gulf War As a Case Study in Media Coverage

Jeff Cohen

February 20, 1991

DB: In the February 17, 1991 *New York Times,* there were two rather extraordinary statements that I would like you to comment on. The first one was by Thomas Friedman, the two-time Pulitzer prize-winning *Times* columnist. He wrote "the image of Iraq as battle-hardened warrior state is largely a myth." In the same edition of the *Times,* R.W. Apple wrote that "during the Iran-Iraq war communiques boasted endlessly about the triumphs and valor of Baghdad's armies. But in fact Iraq's armies were timid, poorly motivated and immobile, with no taste for battle once out from behind their parapets." How does that fit with the popular notion of the juggernaut that Saddam Hussein has created, this massive military machine?

You've picked out two of the *New York Times* leading, most powerful reporters. Thomas Friedman is a virtual sidekick of the man he covers, Secretary of State Jim Baker. They're very close. They bounce ideas off each other. Friedman is the guy who, shortly after Iraq invaded Kuwait, said on one of these morning network TV news shows that what the CIA should consider doing is blowing up some Iraqi pipelines and then lie about having done so. That was a very rare case where a reporter actually asked the government to disinform him. When you see the kinds of truths finally surfacing in the *New York Times* that totally contradict what was being said by Bush and the *New York Times* in the previous months—remember? the buildup toward war on the part of the U.S. propaganda machine that this person is Hitler, his army is the equivalent of Germany's army at the time of Munich; if we don't stop him here he will terrorize the region. And now, after they've gotten us into a war, with the U.S. public believing the mythology of this invincible machine that has to be stopped now because sanctions wouldn't work, it shows the truth of that old adage from Napoleon, that it's not important to suppress the news altogether but to delay it until it no longer matters. Here you had a case where the news was delayed for a period of about six months and finally the *New York Times* is letting us know that compared to many other militaries, especially Western advanced militaries, Iraq isn't really a player. That even the "battle-hardened troops" was exaggerated and exploited.

DB: What was going on in the media in the months before Iraq's invasion on August 2?

We've done a lot of looking back through the 1980s and we're always told by the media after the congressional debate that Americans should feel really good about themselves. The issue of war and peace was thrashed out. It was a full debate, eloquent, impassioned, a full and thorough debate. In fact, the congressional debate was very narrow, and the media hailing it as a full debate shows how narrow the media spectrum is. When you look back at that debate, you see that the Republicans were taking the position that anyone who stands in the way of war was an appeaser akin to Neville Chamberlain, who appeased the Nazis. In a sense, you don't red-bait your opponents any more if you drive toward war, you Neville-bait them. I wrote a column about that. On the other side, the Democrats didn't really have a position to oppose the war.

They had a one-word mantra: sanctions, sanctions, sanctions. Both sides were saying: "In no way should we use diplomacy. In no way should we negotiate. We shouldn't let anyone negotiate." So you had a very narrow debate between sanctions—let's keep squeezing this guy—but let's not budge, let's not try to negotiate. What was important about this narrowness of debate, and how it was hailed in the media as a full debate, is that when the war started on January 16, the *New York Times* had just done a poll. FAIR has always maintained that the debate going on in the country is always broader than the debate in the mainstream media, and that poll showed that the numbers of people who wanted a U.N. peace conference on the Middle East as a way of getting Iraq out of Kuwait were something like 56 percent saying yes, 36 percent saying no. And yet not one pundit during this period got on national TV and said, "Aw, hell, why don't we give in to an international conference and settle this without bloodshed?" That was off the media's agenda. Was it off the agenda because it was so extremist, appeasing Saddam Hussein, that the U.S. public wouldn't stand for such thoughts? Such talk on TV? Of course not. The *New York Times* poll showed that it was a popular position. There was also a narrow majority in the *New York Times* poll that came out at the time of the U.S. attack on Iraq, which showed that most Americans wanted to get the government-in-exile of Kuwait to do a border settlement with Iraq if that would avoid a war. But, of course, you never had a pundit who got on national TV and said, "Why don't we just give them the island, have them lease the island to Iraq, and we can avoid all the bloodshed?" So my point is that the history of the war has always been suppressed in the national media and the debate has always been far narrower. Why? Because the mainstream media rely on the very narrow Washington beltway discussion.

In terms of the longer thrust of your question, the whole history of how the media covered Saddam Hussein:

there was no coverage of his human rights abuses. There
was almost nil. After the crisis began, when the invasion
of Kuwait occurred, all of a sudden he was the greatest
human rights abuser in the world. All of a sudden, Amnesty International reports on Iraq mattered. Those reports were released all through the 1980s, when Iraq was
an ally of the United States, when the Reagan administration took Iraq off the terrorist list so they could give them
billions of dollars in agricultural credits, when the
Reagan-Bush administration was getting guns to Iraq
through third-party states, including Jordan and Kuwait.
During that whole period when the United States was
helping build up the military and economic might of
Saddam Hussein in Iraq, the issue of his human rights
abuses was off the media agenda. There was this classic
in the *New York Post,* a tabloid in New York. After the
crisis began they had a picture of Saddam Hussein patting
the British kid on the head and their banner headline was
"Child Abuser." That was very important to us and very
ironic, because Amnesty International and other human
rights groups had released studies in 1984 and 1985 which
showed that Saddam Hussein's regime regularly tortured
children to get information about their parents, their
parents' views. That just didn't get the coverage. It shows
one of the points that FAIR has made constantly: that
when a foreign government is in favor with the United
States, with the White House, its human rights record is
basically off the mainstream media agenda, and when
they do something that puts them out of favor with the
U.S. government, the foreign government's human rights
abuses are, all of a sudden, major news. It was shocking
to see how little self-criticism there was on the part of the
mainstream media, which was suddenly outraged by this
dictator Saddam Hussein, who they had virtually ignored
for years. The key period in that history was the year and
a half after Bush took power before the invasion of Kuwait, when there were reports in Western media, in West-

ern Europe, that Saddam Hussein was busily trying to get a nuclear trigger and George Bush was doing everything he could to prevent economic sanctions. If we had had a foreign policy that dealt with dictators through diplomacy through the 1980s, instead of building up their economic and military might, there might not ever have been an invasion of Kuwait. Of course, the United States bears large responsibility for that, but that's off the mainstream media agenda. Pundits who have that point of view don't appear. Maybe we should talk about which pundits do appear.

DB: A series of events occurred a week before the Iraqi invasion of Kuwait. I would like you to talk about that.

You're talking about April Glaspie. The signal that was sent to Saddam Hussein by a leading government official named Kelly. April Glaspie, the U.S. Ambassador in Iraq, had a meeting with Saddam Hussein—when intelligence reports were coming in that it looked like the feud between Iraq and Kuwait was going to result in military action by Iraq against Kuwait. She said that the United States would take no position in an Arab-Arab border dispute. While I feel like emphasizing those signals were very important, they've got to be placed in a context of nine years of Reagan-Bush policy. The Reagan-Bush administration was in an alliance with Iraq and it continued during the year and a half after the Iran-Iraq war ended when there was no longer any excuse to help Iraq. George Bush was still protecting Saddam Hussein at a time when he was trying to acquire nuclear triggers. So you put the signal, the green light, that the U.S. government was giving Saddam Hussein right up until the day of the invasion of Kuwait, in the context of the nine years of policy and you will see that there is an incredible foreign policy failure that has gone down the media memory hole. The whole debate in Congress and in the media ignored the history of the issue. You can't bring up nine years of a policy failure for which there now will be a sacrifice of working-class kids. A lot of big companies made a lot of profits from the alliance with Saddam Hussein. The best article on the subject of the alliance with Saddam Hussein was Murray Waases' story in the *Village Voice* called "Gulfgate: How the U.S. Secretly Armed Saddam Hussein."

DB: What do you make of President' Bush's comments that we're going to "put the Vietnam syndrome to rest and we're not going to fight this war with one hand tied behind our back." What is meant by that?

It's not just Bush that says it. You have media pundit after media pundit getting on the air and saying "this time we're going to really fight the war." I heard Robert Shogun, who is the major political writer for the *Los Angeles Times,* say the same thing in his own words. He wasn't quoting a Bush administration official. I think that, with the help of the media, they are doing a lot to put Vietnam and the Vietnam syndrome behind us. War this time isn't something that kills people, at least people that matter, U.S. soldiers. It's more like a Nintendo game. About the myth of one-hand-behind-our-back in Vietnam: the U.S. government poured every weapon imaginable into the war against the Vietnamese people, killing an estimated one million people. A heavy percentage of the people killed were civilians. It was a huge tonnage of bombs. It involved very significant chemical warfare, including Agent Orange. It involved cluster bombs and napalm. The only thing that wasn't dropped on Vietnam was a nuclear bomb. And yet the media myth, the media revisionism, and you see it every day in the paper, is that that was a limited war and that the United States isn't going to make that mistake again. I think what's significant to talk about is why these issues that you and I are discussing don't get into the mainstream media. The mainstream media operate under a code of journalism that's called "objectivity."

The reporters and the anchors can't just go and give a ten-minute spiel of their own opinion. Because of objective journalism, you can't give your own opinion. You have to go to the experts. Since the news from the Persian Gulf War is being censored by every government in the region and comes back to the States in dribs and drabs, television news—and television has been the dominant medium that people turn to in a crisis—has been having expanded coverage. For a long time, the news shows on the networks have been an hour instead of a half-hour. CNN basically has been going around the clock on the Gulf War. What are these TV networks doing? They're parading a series of experts. These experts have been the most one-sided collection of experts that we have seen since we've been tracking TV's pundits and experts since 1986 at FAIR. In fact, in the first weekend, Dennis Miller, the comedic anchorperson for *Saturday Night Live,* got it totally right when he joked, "You know who I really feel sorry for? It's the one retired colonel who didn't get a job as a TV analyst this week." What's odd is that Tom Brokaw, the serious TV anchorperson for NBC news, was introducing two members of an expert panel. First he introduced a retired army colonel. Then he said, "Well, I have to point out that the fairness doctrine is in play here at NBC, so I now want to introduce a retired Navy admiral." This was Tom Brokaw's idea of balance. You have the Army balanced by the Navy. We have tracked who has been getting on and analyzed the real issues. Those experts are conservative thinktank people; generally the Center for Strategic and International Studies has been breaking all records. You've had the retired military analysts, the retired so-called terrorism experts, and, for balance, the Democratic Party representatives, such as Steve Solarz and Les Aspin, who support the war even more strongly than George Bush does. Or, occasionally, you'll have Lee Hamilton, who since the war began said, "I support the war." Basically, you've had no dissent. There aren't any inde-

pendent experts involved in these discussions. Dan Ellsberg was once invited by ABC to appear on a panel
analyzing Secretary of Defense Dick Cheney's briefing of
the press. He was invited by ABC. Why would Dan Ellsberg be an obvious expert if you were engaging in truly
objective and balanced journalism? Because Dan Ellsberg, during the Vietnam War, used to prepare Secretary
of Defense Bob McNamara for his briefings with the press.
So he could give you some real insight. About a half-hour
before Ellsberg was supposed to go on the air on national
news, he was called and told: "That limousine isn't going
to arrive. We've decided not to have you on the panel."
They had two or three hawks and no dissenters. So my
point is that anti-war experts, or independent or critical
experts had not been invited indoors to the table where
the real experts get to discuss the real issues. What has
been shown of the anti-war movement is more in the
nature of outdoors footage, nature footage. It's the anti-
war movement, always outside in its natural habitat, the
street. You would get the impression from watching hours
and hours of television, as we do at FAIR, that anti-war
individuals and experts are incapable of expressing themselves in anything other than a chant or a sound bite or a
slogan. Why? Because they're never invited indoors to
where the real issues are debated. In fact, you have this
debate now—the right wing has been pushing this debate,
as has the Bush administration—about whether the anti-
war movement has been getting too much coverage. The
coverage is always the coverage that marginalizes, that
trivializes, and the experts that you've interviewed for
months, Noam Chomsky, Edward Said, Eqbal Ahmad,
Barbara Ehrenreich, Maxine Waters—the African-Amer-
ican Congresswoman from L.A. who has opposed this war
from Day One—those people don't get invited on national
TV to discuss the issues. If they're ever shown on TV it's
because, like Dan Ellsberg, they've joined an anti-war
march and maybe they will sing a few bars of "Give Peace

a Chance." But that's the kind of national coverage of the anti-war movement we get.

DB: Your organization has issued a couple of very critical reports of MacNeil-Lehrer and Nightline. Let's be specific about the programs now. Have you detected any change in terms of the guests and the ideology that is reflected?

Nightline has always been atrocious. We did a 40-month study and found that the bias of the *Nightline* guest list goes toward the white male conservatives of the military establishment. The four most frequent guests on *Nightline* were Henry Kissinger, Alexander Haig, Elliott Abrams, and Jerry Falwell. Falwell was once asked to give his expertise about AIDS. The *MacNeil-Lehrer Report,*— we did a study of six months of their coverage—is almost as bad as *Nightline,* in some ways worse in excluding public interest experts and excluding people of color and women experts, excluding peace movement experts. Our report on *MacNeil-Lehrer* which was issued last year did so much damage; *MacNeil-Lehrer* prior to our study had an image of being thorough—they're open, they're balanced. We did this study which totally deflated that image of *MacNeil-Lehrer.* An interesting thing happened in the first months of the Persian Gulf crisis. *MacNeil-Lehrer* started sending me notices every time they brought a dissenting person on. It was more than normal. They had Noam Chomsky on for the first time in their history. He got about ten minutes all to himself with Mr. MacNeil. Then the next day they brought Edward Said on for the same treatment, one on one. It was a breakthrough for *MacNeil-Lehrer.* Then they started adding Erwin Knoll, from the *Progressive* magazine, who appeared several times in the months right after the Persian Gulf crisis began. *MacNeil-Lehrer* staffers were basically telling us, "Look, this is a victory for FAIR. These changes that have been made are in many ways because of the constant criticism that we've been getting from you." But then the war began, and as soon as the war began MacNeil-Lehrer went into automatic war pilot. They were just like the old days. They've totally excluded dissenters. I've seen Erwin Knoll on there once. It's been atrocious coverage since January 16.

DB: Let's talk about National Public Radio. The Corporation for Public Broadcasting just issued a grant to NPR for continued war coverage. It called it "superb, exhaustive, the CNN of radio." How do you rate National Public Radio's coverage of the Persian Gulf?

We've been disturbed by National Public Radio, that in fairness to NPR, sometimes they do more in-depth coverage and sometimes a dissenting voice is heard. There was a period where we were monitoring it closely. At the beginning of the war it was appalling. Daniel Schorr kept moderating panels that went from right-wing nuts from the Center for Strategic International Studies and then for balance on the left wing would be Congressperson Solarz or Congressperson Aspin, one of the Democrats who supports the war more strongly than Bush does. I remember a panel on Day Two of the war. Daniel Schorr thought it was such an important panel. He had two representatives from the right-wing think tank, the Center for Strategic International Studies and they were balanced by Senator McCain, a right-wing Republican from Arizona. Some of their panels are so bankrupt and so imbalanced that the word "public" in their title is really obscene. If you're really engaging in public broadcasting you cannot exclude from your list of experts minority and dissenting points of view, and it should be pointed out that since the beginning of this crisis there has been a very strong gender gap, where women have been far more opposed to the war than men. We always heard in the media about the so-called "national consensus" behind President Bush. That consensus never included African

Americans and Arab Americans. So if you're engaging in public broadcasting you have to have dissenting voices and racial minority voices and women voices. They just don't do a good enough job on NPR.

DB: Martin Lee and Norman Solomon in their book, *Unreliable Sources,* talk about journalists today as being stenographers and not really journalists, not reporters. Why is that?

It's a trend that's gone on for many years since that blip in time known as Watergate, where reporters in Washington, the Washington press corps has grown closer and closer to its sources. It's to the point where Brit Hume, the ABC correspondent at the White House, plays tennis with George Bush. Tom Friedman of the *New York Times* is very close with Jim Baker. You find these relationships are so close that reporters don't challenge the subjects of their stories, they just tell you what the government is saying. In other words, they've become stenographers for power and not journalists. There are classic examples of this. George Bush keeps making statements, that any bush league reporter knows are one-sided, when he keeps invoking international law. Not once has a mainstream reporter on national TV said, "Well, it was a major violation of international law when Bush invaded Panama." When Bush constantly invokes the "family of nations" and that the U.N. is united against Iraq, it's not pointed out by any of these mainstream journalists (and it would be if they were acting as journalists and not stenographers) that President Bush didn't admit that the invasion of Panama was declared, in an overwhelming vote at the U.N., a grievous violation of international law. Another example of reporters acting as stenographers is the issue we talked about earlier, where Bush says that we aren't going to fight this one with one hand behind our back as we did with Vietnam. No one goes on record and says, "I covered Vietnam and the only thing not dropped on Vietnam was a nuclear bomb."

DB: Let's talk about the use of pronouns, which flows out of what you were just talking about. Bob Edwards, for example, the anchor on NPR's Morning Edition, invariably invokes "we" and "our." "What are we going to do if Iraq does this?" "How shall our forces respond?" What is that reflective of?

It's reflective of a media that is no longer separate from the state. One of the slogans I've heard at demonstrations outside the *New York Times* and the TV networks is: "Two-four-six-eight, separate the press and state." We've seen Judy Woodruff talk about "How well are we doing, our armed forces?" I didn't notice that she was wearing a Marines uniform. Independent press is supposed to talk about the Marines and the Pentagon in the third person. They aren't supposed to be speaking about the Pentagon or the U.S. armed forces as "we." We've been able to document dozens of examples where anchorpeople and national TV correspondents put questions like this: "How long is it going to take us to lick this guy? How long is it going to take us to defeat him?" Besides the "we" there's the other pronoun problem: "him." What the media have done is to pick up the lingo of the Pentagon. They've made it seem, day after day in the TV news, that we are fighting an individual. You don't fight wars against individuals. You fight boxing matches against individuals, you fight duels, but wars are fought against nations. There are thousands of civilians who have died. When you have the media constantly personifying the war: "How long is it going to take us to lick him? How uncomfortable is he?" Saddam Hussein is probably the one person in Iraq who's eating three square meals a day. He's probably the safest person in Iraq. When you have the media falling for that kind of rhetoric, that we're only

hurting one person, we're punishing one person, you have
them basically going for a ride with the Pentagon. You've
had these other kinds of quotes from the national media,
where they say how the strategy of aerial bombardment
has been a strategy to keep casualties down. Tom Brokaw
said that word for word. What Brokaw meant is that the
massive air bombardment strategy was a way of keeping
U.S. casualties down. They were trying to keep casualties
down so they could keep U.S. protest down so they could
keep the war going. When you have people talking about
"casualties" and you look closely at their story and you
realize that all they're talking about is U.S. soldiers, then
you're seeing a lot of jingoism and racism. Newsweek had
the most ironic cover story. It was puff piece about the
high-tech weapons, in Newsweek on February 18. The
cover title was: "The New Science of War. High-Tech
Warfare—How Many Lives Can It Save?" Ironically, this
was out on the newsstands when the U.S. bombs destroyed hundreds of Iraqi civilians in a bomb shelter. The
title of the Newsweek article read "How Many Lives Can
It Save?" I read the article closely and it became clear. The
only lives that Newsweek was concerned about were those
of U.S. soldiers. The idea that Arab civilian casualties
should be of any concern to a Newsweek reader was
beyond the writers of that article.

DB: In terms of the personalization that goes on in
the media, you've cited examples of Saddam Hussein;
what about Noriega, Qaddafi, Maurice Bishop, Ayatollah
Khomeini—is there a pattern there?

We used to clock Ted Koppel, the most influential TV
journalist. I remember when it looked like there might
threaten to be a peace with Nicaragua and a regional
peace, and the contras might have to lay down their arms;
I remember Ted Koppel interrogating Aronsen, the
spokesperson for the Reagan-Bush administration on the

contras. The question he kept asking was, "How are we going to make Daniel Ortega pay? How does this punish Ortega?" It's typical of the news media. We didn't punish Ortega. The U.S. government is responsible for killing tens of thousands of Nicaraguan civilians. It's typical of the macho media elite to make it seem like wars are just fought between heads of state, because, especially in the case of Koppel, all he deals with is heads of state. One thing that we should talk about, because we talked about it earlier, about objective journalism, is how expert have these pundits have been. At FAIR we have the slogan, "the more off you are, the more on you are." In other words, the more inaccurate you are, the more television time you get. The classic case was the one question that the media was concerning itself with in January: How long is it going to take us to lick this guy? How long will the war last? You had, for example, on the *McLaughlin Group,* which rarely has a broad spectrum of views, but what was their spectrum of views on predicting how long the war would last? This was the first weekend after the war began. The optimists said it would take thirteen days for the war to end. The pessimists said it could last a full three weeks. That was the total spectrum. After the three weeks ended, we communicated to McLaughlin that we thought that since these five pundits had revealed themselves to be utterly inept, that maybe they should replace these five and hire five new experts who really know what they're talking about. You had a parade of experts like former CIA director William Colby, who assured us the war would be over in an afternoon. You had a right-wing Congressperson, Robert Dornan, who is a fixture on CNN; and I think CNN, like NPR, gets a lot of praise that is undeserved. They have the same narrow spectrum of experts. Robert Dornan got on CNN and said, this war will take two days. The most important figure in getting George Bush the votes he needed to start the war was Democratic Congressperson Les Aspin from Wisconsin. Les Aspin was on television networks so often during December and January that we were wondering whether he had a television union card. He was going from network to network, and what was he saying? Especially on CBS's America Tonight, the competitor show with Nightline. He said, this war will take weeks, not months; he said that over and over. He said, we may not even need a ground war. We can do this from the air. What was interesting was, a couple of weeks into the war, Associated Press had a story they sent out across the country quoting Les Aspin prominently, saying, President Bush isn't doing a good job preparing the U.S. public for the large number of casualties there will be when the ground war begins. It struck me that the Associated Press was acting as a stenographer to power. When Les Aspin was saying this war will be over in no time, he was in every media outlet to say that unquestioned. When he came on later and said this war could be very dangerous, it could bog down, it could cost thousands of U.S. troops, the stenographers in the mainstream media just put that out and never once did a reporter say to Les Aspin, well, wait a second. You're largely responsible for getting us into this war on the basis that it would take weeks and might not even need a ground war. So how can you now be saying something totally different?

DB: Senator Alan Simpson of Wyoming has described Peter Arnett of CNN, who is reporting from Baghdad, as an "enemy sympathizer." How do you evaluate Arnett's reporting from Iraq?

Arnett's reporting has, I think, been essential. It's been one of the few bright spots. Correctly, CNN tells you that his stories are cleared by censors. What's ironic is that many of the stories that appear on CNN are cleared by censors, but it's only Arnett's stories where you get a big lead-in on how this was cleared by Iraqi censors. It's always flashed on the screen: Cleared by Iraqi censors, and then after the story ends you hear it again. I don't think that's that bad, but I'd like to see that same kind of talk about the Pentagon censorship, which is massive. Arnett, of course, has given us a window into what's happening inside Iraq. It's an important window for the U.S. public to see because, as I said, wars, despite what the media pundits say, are not fought against individuals. They kill all sorts of innocent civilians. The person who shed the best light on this is one of the best columnists in our country writing for one of the better newspapers, *New York Newsday*, and that's Murray Kempton. Kempton pointed out that what's really being shown by this war is that the weapons of modern warfare are just too horrible, that wars are obsolete, that there's got to be a better way. Kempton pointed out that 80 percent of the victims of wars since World War II have been civilians. It's such an obvious point. The fact that Murray Kempton is off-key saying that in a column in *Newsday* and that kind of point is never made in the more national media says something about how narrow the perspectives are in the national media. We've gone through this before in Panama. That was an air war, an air bombardment. All the media concerned itself with was, how many U.S. soldiers have died? Kathleen Sullivan of CBS got on TV nearly crying. "Eight U.S. soldiers have died. How long can this fighting go on?" By the point that she was grieving about the eight U.S. soldiers, it's very likely that a thousand Panamanian civilians had been baked in their homes in the El Chorrillo section of Panama City. The point is that it took nine months before a national network, CBS, did a *Sixty Minutes* story on the full range of civilian casualties. But during the time that the Panama invasion was going on, all we heard from the national media was: *We* are doing so well. This is one of the most successful U.S. military operations in years. I think the Pentagon, from their Panama experience, felt they could count on the ignoring of civilian casualties in the Persian Gulf War. Given the history of lies about civilian casualties in Vietnam, in Panama, the continual lying now about civilian casualties in Iraq, the way the media constantly falls for it, they almost invert the words in the song by the rock group The Who: "We *Will* Be Fooled Again." In the mainstream media, no matter what has gone before, they are eternally gullible when the Pentagon gives them numbers or tells them how smart and how accurate our bombs are. We heard all about the surgical strikes in Panama and what the nurses and ambulance drivers in Panama City were saying. Surgical strikes? Those are strikes by the United States that send our people to surgery wards, that's what a surgical strike is.

DB: Clearly there's a pattern emerging here, starting with Grenada and Panama and now the Persian Gulf, of U.S. control of the news. If what you're saying is accurate, that the press is so compliant and obsequious, why do they even have to go through the machinations of censorship?

That's a good question. I would argue that the worst reporting in the U.S. media is not the reporting that's been censored. Some of that reporting has been real lame. They interviewed the Marines and the pilots who are all gung-ho, "We kicked ass today." No soldier is going to talk candidly to a reporter in Saudi Arabia; every reporter has a military escort who's usually a higher-ranking officer than the soldier who's being interviewed. No one is going to say, "I'm scared. I wish I wasn't here." You would never say that, because of the censorship. But I would argue that even with those negatives in the reports that come from the war theater, the worst reporting on television is the reporting from New York and Washington. That's been the most biased. That's been the steady parade of hawks, the Center for Strategic and International Studies debating another conservative think tank, American Enterprise. I remember the *Nightline* panel, this had nothing to do with Pentagon censorship. They had: representing the right wing, Patrick Buchanan; representing the center Newt Gingrich; and representing the left was a Democratic party Congressman who was saying, "I'm rallying 'round the President." I'm supporting the war. It was three war hawks. I would argue that the most bias in the U.S. media—and it's the bias that people are glued to—is the bias that comes out of the studio with the one-sided parade of experts, and the Pentagon isn't censoring that. That's journalists making a decision that they are going to censor anti-war perspectives or independent perspectives.

DB: If, as you say, truth and accuracy are taking a beating in this kind of coverage, it seems that the English language is under assault, too. You have "aircraft going out on sorties, delivering their ordnance to soften up targets, and there may be some collateral damage but a BDA (bomb damage assessment) will determine that later."

Noam Chomsky has talked about this since the Vietnam War. The way the Pentagon has prostituted the English language toward its ends, when concentration camps were called "strategic hamlets" and "pacification programs" in Vietnam. The thing that I keep hearing is the "smart bombs" and the "surgical strikes." There is so much evidence to the contrary, and yet the U.S. reporters still pick up that lingo from the Pentagon.

DB: Talk if you will about polls, because polls seem to be very, very critical in the formulation and application of national policy. How are questions designed, and who asks those questions?

In mid-February, for example, when the Soviets were pushing toward peace (not just the Soviets; there were other countries which wanted to avert a further war

and an escalation of the war). Poll after poll—we saw this
in the *New York Times,* in *Newsday,* all the Gallup polls—
was asking this question: Do you think U.S. and allied
forces should begin a ground attack soon to drive the
Iraqis out of Kuwait, or should we hold off for now and
continue to rely on air power to do the job? If you are one
who believes that too many civilians have died already,
that we're bombing Iraq into the 19th century and there's
a way for the U.S. government through diplomacy, to
accomplish its goals of getting Iraq out of Kuwait without
this war, you had no answer. It was one of those questions:
Do you support the ground war or do you support the air
war? If you're one who supports neither war, you had to
add yourself to the "uninformed" or uncaring "I don't
know. I don't have an opinion." We've been tracking these
poll questions. People should be very suspicious of polling
data. By the way, we should talk about not taking the
media lying down. If you are a consumer of news and you
are appalled by the steady stream of white male conservative war hawks, then it's your duty as someone who
cares about democracy to pick up a phone, write a letter,
fax a letter and demand that the media be balanced. When
you see a poll that you're skeptical about, call the newspaper and say, can you send me the raw data. It's usually
ten pages where they write up what the full questions
were, what the votes were, how many the don't-know's
were. I remember a doozie from the *Los Angeles Times*
before the war started. It read: "If Hussein pulls his troops
out of all Kuwait, should the United States keep a military
presence in the Persian Gulf to maintain stability in the
region or not?" Of course, the question assumed that U.S.
military forces maintain stability in the region. By the
way, the *Los Angeles Times* is considered very respectable.
The *Times-Mirror* polls are always reprinted in papers
across the country. If you believe that a permanent or
semi-permanent U.S. presence in the Middle East would
be hurtful to regional stability, you could have phrased

the question: If Hussein pulls his troops out of all Kuwait, should the United States keep a military presence in the Persian Gulf or remove them in the interest of regional stability? If you frame the question that way, overwhelmingly the U.S. public would have said, no, let's get the U.S. troops out. I feel that the public is snookered by biased questions. The consuming public should be very skeptical about those questions.

DB: One of the burning issues in this whole debate has revolved around the issue of "linkage." How has that been treated in the mainstream media?

It goes with the coverage of the Middle East in the mainstream media going back years. You would not know from the mainstream media that there's been an international consensus on the Middle East, including the Western European countries, that there should be two states, side by side, a Palestinian state and an Israeli state. The overwhelming weight of authority in the world, the consensus in the world, is that there should be negotiations between Israel and the PLO. You wouldn't know that from the U.S. media. You'd think that's controversial. So you've had this war starting because George Bush under no circumstances would consent to an international peace conference on the Middle East. What's interesting is that in the media, one institution, perhaps even more than the Pentagon, has risen in the mainstream media in this country as "coming back." It's getting all this propaganda. What institution is it? It's the United Nations. The mainstream media look at the United Nations very selectively. On November 29, when Bush got the authorization he wanted to have a deadline where the use of force would be possible against Iraq, that was major news. There were all these accolades for the U.N. The very next day another vote was taken. It was a vote you didn't hear much about in the mainstream media, called "Question of Palestine."

It was a vote on whether there should be an international Middle East peace conference, on whether Israel should pull out of the Palestinian territories. What was the vote? 144 to 2. The dissenting votes were, as usual, the United States and Israel. So it's not known in this country how strong the international consensus is for an international peace conference, nor is it known that the U.S. public overwhelmingly supports an international peace conference on the Middle East and that the *New York Times* poll the day the war started was 56 percent to 37 percent in favor of such a conference. So I think it's only by excluding certain facts from the discussion that George Bush could get on TV day after day and say: "Linkage—not prudent. Won't tolerate it. Unconditional" and get away with it. The public wasn't even informed that the idea of a conference is very popular with the public. The idea that Iraq could have been gotten out of Kuwait without a war, through an international peace conference, was overwhelmingly supported by the U.S. public. Not one TV pundit raised that issue.

DB: As you survey the scene of corporate-dominated media, what bright spots are there, if any, and what alternatives are there? How can one start a network, for example, a TV network or a newspaper? What's that famous quote from A.J. Liebling, "Anyone's free to open up a newspaper just as long as they have ten million dollars?"

The other quote is, "freedom of the press belongs to those who own one." In fact, there are some alternatives. The papers like the *Village Voice*, the *L.A. Weekly*, are alternative weeklies that have really covered the issue well from the beginning of the crisis on August 2. They've brought out all of these histories, all of the history at the U.N., the history of the international consensus on a Middle East peace conference, the history of the alliance.

It wasn't appeasement, the alliance between Reagan-Bush and Saddam Hussein. Those issues have been well covered. Also on Pacifica radio, in *Z* magazine, in *The Nation* magazine, in *In These Times*. There is this alternative media that wasn't really there around Vietnam. There was an underground media during Vietnam, but it wasn't as professional. It wasn't doing the hard digging. It wasn't as sound in terms of fact-checking and historical digging. There are a lot of alternatives. What's interesting to me is the way the U.S. television networks constantly parade their one-sided propaganda, their cheerleading for the war, their boosterism for the Pentagon and all the smart bombs and high-tech technology and then they poll the public: What do you think of the war? Any time anything slips in about civilian casualties, very quickly to follow will be the word "propaganda" or "manipulation" or "propaganda windfall for Saddam Hussein." In the context of that very propagandistic coverage, they are always polling the public and saying, well, the public continues to support the war, 80 percent. Frankly, what they're doing is gauging the power of their own propaganda. It's not sound to continually poll the U.S. public until you've provided them with alternative or differing points of view or wide-ranging debate. What FAIR is doing nationally is mobilizing media consumers to no longer be intimidated consumers. And it's succeeding. We know that thousands of letters and calls have been made to the national TV networks complaining about the failure to include independent analysts in the news where the real experts sit. We at FAIR and other groups even had a demonstration in New York. We started at NBC, marched over to PBS and went to CBS and ended at ABC, where Peter Jennings, the anchorperson, came down and talked to the protesters for about 35 minutes in a very good discussion where he heard our complaints about media use of the pronoun "we" and failure to include anti-war perspectives as experts, not out in the street, not protesting and chanting, but bringing in the leaders of that movement to debate the Kissingers and the Haigs. So the mobilization to demand media balance has never been more intense. It's in a sense a new thing leading to people like Peter Jennings coming downstairs and actually meeting their critics. It's the only hope. Your track should be twofold: One, you fight the mainstream media to end the censorship and you demand balancing viewpoints; and two, you support the alternative media that goes into depth on issues that the mainstream media will glance over in a ten-second story. Those are the two tracks, and frankly I'm optimistic that both are working better than ever. I've never been more proud of the alternative media than in their coverage of the Persian Gulf. I'm talking not just radio, community radio, but the print publications and television. The Gulf Crisis TV Project, done by Deep Dish, which was sent up on satellite and pulled down by cable access stations across the country as well as some PBS stations, that was a monumental achievement in independent journalism, alternative journalism. That's going great. Then there's this new thing, where never before have media consumers—I know African Americans are complaining to the media like mad. Women's groups are circulating letters saying, why aren't there women who get to debate foreign policy? Bella Abzug has been one of these. She leads a group of women concerned about foreign policy. Never before has so much well-informed criticism been leveled at the media, the criticism taken directly to the mainstream journalists. In the past, especially public interest activists and environmentalist and peace activists, what they'd do when they saw bad media is they complained to each other, instead of taking their intelligent and serious complaints to the media who are doing the censoring, and that's changing. So I'm optimistic on both counts.

DB: So, how should people react to the media?

We have found that the main message we can bring to an audience is: Don't take the media lying down. It's not enough to grumble quietly to oneself about media bias. If there's an aroused public, we have found at FAIR, you can exert an influence even on the media owned by General Electric. We've demonstrated it. We've had victories. We know that there are programs which got on PBS that never would have gotten on except for FAIR's work and the work of other activists. We know that stories have been published in the *New York Times* about the death squads in Honduras, for example, that they probably wouldn't have bothered with except that we were putting so much heat on them for scrutinizing minor human rights infractions in Nicaragua and placing that on the front page while ignoring major death squad activities in neighboring countries. So there are successes that FAIR can point to and we just ask people to join. We are a membership organization. All members receive our bi-monthly publication called *Extra*. We look at the news that's not in the news and we look at the gaffes. We talk about the themes that the media keep propounding which may be bogus themes, and mostly we talk about the issues they never talk about. We just believe that if you're going to be an informed citizen you have to look at a variety of sources. That's the key to getting the news. Don't rely on one media source, especially if it's one that's owned by a big corporation, like General Electric owning NBC when it's General Electric weaponry in part that is being used in the Gulf War. General Electric stands to gain from future wars. I would be skeptical of what I see on NBC because of GE's ownership.

And be skeptical of the alternative media. Alternative media is advocacy journalism, and you can get a good mix, and then I think you and the American public can find your way to truth. That's all we advocate at FAIR.

The Gulf War and the Media

Alexander Cockburn

June 4, 1991

DB: You know the timeworn cliché, "Truth is the first casualty of war." How did truth fare in the recently concluded Gulf War?

About as badly as usual. In almost all aspects of the war the journalism was predictably pretty incompetent or mendacious, or a mixture of both.

DB: Given the political economy of the media, could one expect anything else in terms of the quality of the coverage?

Not really. The startling difference, as usual, was from country to country. I spent a lot of the war in Ireland reading the *International Herald Tribune,* which is a mixture of the *New York Times* and the *Washington Post* mostly, and the English and Irish papers. I have to say that the Irish papers were probably the best, because the Irish, having been through many centuries of being on the receiving end of colonial exploitation, simply have a different attitude. Of all the journalism—and I say this with a certain amount of subjective interest—probably the best reporting, not editorializing, was done by *The Independent,* the British paper, by my brother Patrick, who was in Baghdad, and Bob Fisk, who was in Saudi Arabia, both of whom have been in the Middle East for a very long time.

DB: A number of people were very critical of the BBC coverage of the Gulf crisis and war. Did you have an opportunity to listen to any of the BBC reports?

Yes. It wasn't very good. I listened to the World Service every day. In the Thatcher years there had been an attack on the BBC, particularly the World Service. At the beginning of this war there was a tremendous onslaught against the BBC. I think it did have an effect. The reporting just simply wasn't particularly good. By and large, the censorship and fear of censorship were pretty effective around the world among the U.S.-led coalition countries. Take Australia. I did quite a lot of phone interviews with ABC [Australian Broadcasting Corporation]. They have a late night program there. They told me it was the only program that had any critical commentary on the war. They had Noam Chomsky, me, Fisk from Saudi Arabia, Christopher Hitchens. They came under onslaught in the Australian parliament, also a direct attack on their funding. I don't know about the Canadian Broadcasting Corporation (CBC) coverage. It's usually better than most of the U.S. stuff. And there are areas that I think have not received as much attention as they should. One of the major extraordinary things was the fact that at the onset of the bombing, with the exception of CNN and NBC, almost all of the U.S. press corps in Baghdad ran away. No one's made much of this, but in my view it's an extraordinary scandal. You had a very large U.S. press corp in Baghdad, and in the days immediately preceding the bombing, which began on the 17th, they all left. They left partly at the urging of their publishers and editors, partly on their own initiative, generally under the pressure of the U.S. administration, claiming that they thought Baghdad was going to be leveled in the bombing. Of course, if everyone had followed suit, this would have left no one to witness what happened. This, to me, is a scandal which very little has been made of.

DB: Did you have occasion to watch CNN and Peter Arnett's coverage of the Gulf War in particular, and the comments from General Schwarzkopf and Senator Simpson that he was a collaborator and an enemy sympathizer?

Yes, I saw that. It was good that Arnett remained. I think the famous first broadcast on the first night showed all the limitations of TV "live" coverage, which really showed nothing. But the fact that Arnett came under this pressure from Senator Simpson, obviously at the instigation of the administration, showed how resentful the administration was of the fact that CNN had stayed.

DB: In your view, did the media promote the notion that the war was unavoidable?

Yes, very much so. This was particularly clear in the handling of the matter of negotiations or the non-reporting of what negotiations were going on. The record has been increasingly established now that there were Iraqi overtures in early August which continued toward the end. You can say that they were fake and bogus and Saddam Hussein was just fooling around, but they should have been tested. They weren't tested, and one of the reasons they weren't and the Bush administration got away with not testing them, proceeding straightforwardly towards the war, was that the press didn't pick them up. There were certain notable exceptions, like Knut Royce of *Newsday,* which did run a number of stories.

DB: Grenada, Libya, Panama, Iraq. Over all of these bombings, invasions and wars looms the specter of Vietnam and the notion that somehow the media were responsible for the loss of that war.

This obviously has been encouraged by one administration after another, by the Right and by the media themselves. Anyone studying the press coverage of the Vietnam War would have found out instantly that they weren't particularly critical. The first editorial attacking the war didn't come until late 1967, from the *Boston Globe*. For most of the war, up until its very end, the media were generally extremely supportive. But, of course, successive administrations and the Right have used the charge of treachery to cow the press and kick it towards total submission. To go back to this business about it being inevitable: when Bush began to claim that sanctions had failed, long before the sanctions conceivably could have really worked, there was no real scrutiny.

DB: I was recently in New Orleans, where there was a conference of National Public Radio broadcasters. I had an opportunity to challenge a panel. I have to tell you that these people got standing ovations for NPR's coverage of the war. I stood up and suggested to them that they were indeed following the administration agenda about the Gulf in terms of whether the United States had great concerns for human rights, fidelity to international law, devotion to the U.N., etc. and that they didn't cover the real issues of the war, like the politics of oil. One of the panelists said, "Didn't you hear that one program that John Idste did in October about oil?" as if that one five or ten minute story was enough to provide that crucial balance.

This is always true. *MacNeil-Lehrer* can say they had Chomsky on for ten minutes in September, or had Edward Said on briefly. Or with newspapers: you can't say they never did this or never did that. There's always a little piece or five minutes on TV tucked away somewhere. After the beginning of the actual bombing war, even that tiny corrective amount of information or commentary was immediately cut off. That's how they get away with it. You allow this one tiny "cheep" in a torrent of rubbish. Then the NPR people will point, saying: We did that, we did this.

DB: You had an exchange, in fact, in the June 10, 1991 issue of *The Nation,* with Jeff Cohen, Executive Director of Fairness and Accuracy in Reporting (FAIR) in New York. You quote a reader who wrote to you who said, "FAIR is a bit off the mark if they think just getting Chomsky on once for ten minutes on *MacNeil-Lehrer* is somehow going to correct this enormous imbalance and bias in the media."

Yes, it was a good point. I'd had a little glancing comment about FAIR in something I had written, where I said that I thought FAIR was falling into the trap of calling for the media to be objective, whereas there is no such thing as objectivity, in my view. To start addressing the U.S. corporate media in terms of objectivity is ludicrous. There's always an inherent, inbuilt tilt towards the priorities of property and capital and so forth. Therefore you're always playing on a tilted playing field. I think everybody at FAIR knows this perfectly well, but I think sometimes their rhetoric encourages the idea that there is a genuinely level playing field and if you chip away at the resistance of the editors and producers and so forth you'll end up with this level playing field, which is dangerous nonsense. You should push away, but basically the real effort should be in trying to establish independent institutions. I think the war really demonstrated that. When the real bombing war started, people like Chomsky could get nowhere near *MacNeil-Lehrer* or NPR or whatever. That's when you turn to stations like yours, or Pacifica, or BAI, or alternative newspapers. We've got to try to build those up as much as possible.

DB: Given the acute lack of capital and resources, how is that realistically going to happen?

It's a problem. It's always been a problem. I think people have to make the effort to try to start local papers.

There should be a real push to try to get low-watt radios, community-based radios, which the FCC and the police constantly hassle and harass. There are people I know trying to stitch together some kind of left-wing cable network. I think it would be a terrible battle even to get to the starting post, because it requires enormous sums of capital and dealing with cable operators who will double-cross you at every turn. But that kind of push has to go on. At the same time, of course, it's not a bad idea to try to pressure *MacNeil-Lehrer* into putting on something other than utterly conventional opinion.

DB: There are now a plethora of books critiquing the mainstream media: by Parenti, Bagdikian, Chomsky and Herman, Hertsgaard, Schiller, Lee and Solomon, your book *Corruptions of Empire,* but so what? Has there been any change in terms of impact now that there's this body of literature?

I don't think there's been much of a change at all. I speak for myself, but when I write my stuff and attack coverage of, say, Central America, the Middle East, the absence of comment on labor, I don't expect the objects of my criticism to mend their ways at all. It's more political education for people. At least that's how I see it, and I imagine that's how most people who do it see it. I can't imagine that Noam Chomsky and Ed Herman think that the editor of the *New York Times* will wake up one day and say, "My God, I've read Chomsky and Herman and now I realize that I've been running the ship wrong!" It's a way to disclose to people how facts are manipulated or invented and how the political agenda of the ruling elites is established. I think that's good. Obviously, the vacuum is the absence of political formations. The effort always is to change, to alter consciousness. But there's got to be a correlative in the form of political formations. That's obviously where the gap is, although I think there are some encouraging signs. Press criticism in the absence of a political party is ultimately only one hand clapping. In formations such as Central American and solidarity movements a lot of people read my stuff, and it was for them that a lot of my work is done. This was a continuing service just to keep people up to date on the lies. It's useful for them, for people organizing for Central America and elsewhere, if they can take an article I've done in the *Wall Street Journal* or wherever it happens to be, and hand it to someone and say, "Look, here are the lies." It's useful in that way.

DB: But when you're writing for that audience, in *The Nation* and *In These Times* and the *Los Angeles Times Weekly*, etc., aren't you preaching to the converted to some extent?

Yes, you are to a certain extent. But the converted need information on an ongoing basis. There's no question about it. And, one hopes, you're attracting more people with your persuasive words as you do it. But the converted are very important. If you leave the converted alone long enough, or bore them with stupid or casual journalism, maybe they'll stop being converted and relapse into indifference or other undesirable states.

DB: Let's talk a little bit more about the Gulf War and the media coverage of it. If in fact the media are closely aligned with the state, why then the elaborate efforts to control and manage them, in the Gulf specifically, the pool coverage, the minders in the field, the censorship, etc.? And why did they go along with it?

I think they went along with it because—and they admit this now—they went along with a gradual increase in censorship, starting with Grenada, then Panama, and finally this. They accepted an increasingly rigorous system. Actually, the Pentagon needn't have bothered as much as they did, considering what these reporters were likely to do anyway. But there are real limitations to what you can find out. One should also recognize that. Take the case of the hailed and vaunted Patriot missile. It now turns out that the Patriot missile was a miserable failure. The casualties in Israel increased after they deployed the Patriot. The failure rates were enormous. Maybe there should have been one journalist with sufficient access inside the Pentagon to discover the true talk about how the weapons were doing. Certainly there were scientists available to present a different story. There has been remarkably little even now, when it's fairly well known that the failure rates were fairly high and a lot of these weapons didn't work very well. *The Nation* made extraordinary claims for a so-called new generation of weapons which were near-nuclear in capacity. First of all, it's untrue. Secondly, I think the Left loves to frighten itself with talk of superweapons and incredibly competent weapons. They did this with the electronic battlefield stuff in Vietnam. Most of the time these weapons weren't working very well. Of course, they were killing people, but for their specific military tasks they weren't working particularly well. Schwarzkopf was right when he said the two sides could have exchanged weapons and the results would have been the same.

There were extraordinary stories, like that of Bob Fisk, the reporter for *The Independent,* who didn't have a pool pass and got around Saudi Arabia and around the areas of coalition deployment just by hitching rides with troops. When an NBC guy spotted him during Khafji, he called the military police over and said, you're not meant to be here and ordered them to arrest him and take him away. This is the level to which most of the U.S. press had reduced itself.

DB: Fisk was involved in another incident in liberated Kuwait. He came across a scene of some Kuwaitis beating up Palestinians.

As I recall it, Fisk reported that he and Colin Smith of *The Observer* saw some Kuwaitis beating up a Palestinian boy. While they were rescuing the boy from this situation, a U.S. Special Forces captain or major came up and told them that they didn't want their sort around here, journalists making trouble, and told them to "fuck off." It's an interesting story, because it shows that at that point the U.S. Special Forces were working very carefully with the Kuwaitis, who were persecuting and rounding up these wretched people and torturing them. I will say that, in the wake of the war, particularly in the *L.A. Times,* the reporting from Kuwait has been pretty good.

DB: What do you attribute that to?

I think a number of papers did feel that they had somehow become part of an avalanche during the war and felt guilty afterwards. That they were somehow swept away and they're trying to recoup a bit of their dignity. But clearly, what matters is the period when they had been swept away. That's the dangerous period, what I always call the electronic Nuremberg rally, when suddenly all dissent is leached out of the system. The *L.A. Times* is, by and large, a better paper, partly because it's out of the Washington-New York policy loop. Now they're giving each other prizes, like they gave a Pulitzer Prize to that woman from the *Washington Post* who was in Kuwait for a month, Caryle Murphy. If you actually go back and read what she was writing, it was awful, boring, stupid stuff, but they gave her a Pulitzer Prize and patted themselves on the back. Appalling spectacle.

DB: You were involved in exposing the infamous incubator atrocity story. What first alerted you that this may have been a "cruel hoax," as George Bush would say?

The story began to surface in the fall. What was being described was Iraqi soldiers tossing babies out of their incubators, taking the incubators away to be sent back to Baghdad. It seemed to me even then that that bore all the hallmarks of your classic untrue atrocity story, remarkably similar to stories which were put out by British propaganda in the First World War about Germans killing babies and throwing them up and catching them on their bayonets. You want to read these stories pretty carefully. Then I noticed that this was circulated by the Kuwait government-in-exile, as you might expect. They wanted to discredit the Iraqis as much as they could. Then it was given really serious currency in the Amnesty report in November and December. I was reading a Middle East Watch report, testimony by Andrew Whitley, the director of Middle East Watch, to Congress, and he didn't mention the incubator stuff. This struck me as odd, because this was, after all, supposedly an incredible atrocity, over 300 babies. This is up there with Deir Yassin or something like that. I looked about a bit and discovered that some human rights investigators didn't think that the story stood up. By that time it turned out that Amnesty's major witness was a Red Crescent official. Red Crescent officials in Kuwait are in the pay of the government, so he was actually an employee of the government-in-exile and was staying in the Taif Sheraton, which is where the royal family was in exile. And he had changed his story already. So it was clear that he was fairly suspect. Actually, when you read it all carefully, it was clear even from what they were saying that it was hearsay. When you stopped to think about it, it was obviously ridiculous. If you took a baby out of an incubator and threw it on a floor, if you did this to a lot of babies, they wouldn't all die immediately. At least some of these poor little things would take a long time to die. This is meant to happen in a hospital, where there were doctors and nurses? The reports didn't say they took the babies out and killed them, just that they put them on the floor. So it began to look bogus. Then it turned out that a lot of doctors and nurses, who had been in Kuwait and left after the alleged atrocity, said it wasn't true. I wrote this up, and the American Amnesty International people, Healey & Co., showed disgusting behavior. They began to say that I—they didn't say me, but there was only one person who was criticizing this story—was denying Iraqi atrocities in Kuwait, which I certainly wasn't doing. Finally, in March, the press—ABC did it most thoroughly—interviewed all the people, whom they could have interviewed in November, because the crucial witnesses were in Cairo and London at the time, and they finally got around to saying it was all nonsense. Bush cited the story six times in the month preceding the bombing war. It was an indicator atrocity story.

DB: The other big story during the bombing campaign, excuse me, the sorties that delivered ordnance—we could talk, too, about the Orwellian use of language that was crystallized during this war—was the bombing of the shelter. Of course, when Iraqis take shelter it's called a "bunker," sort of reminds one of Hitler, doesn't it?

Yes, the whole bunker-shelter business. I think that was a real test. Once liberals swallowed that one, they'd swallow anything. I remember reading a column by Charles Krauthammer in which he said that, for a lot of people on the home front and not out there fighting, the way they could really demonstrate their support of the bombing war was by supporting the bombing of the shelter. I could scarcely believe my eyes. Krauthammer is a particularly disgusting individual. Remember, this was a situation where cameras are photographing incinerated victims, mostly women and small children, and the *New York Times* runs a piece, I think from Brinkley, filed in Israel, quoting Israel "experts" as saying they can see from the photographs that the survivors in the hospital were clearly faking it. Can you imagine the mentality that could run stories like that? That was a sign that the press was *completely* captured by the government at that point. Followed by the statement, insisting that it was a military facility. There were interviews available with the people who constructed the shelter, saying, no, it's not a bunker, it was always a shelter. Then they began to say that the Rashid Hotel itself was over a military bunker, which made me think that they were quite prepared to bomb the Rashid if it came to it.

DB: You're probably familiar with the incident tangential to this, of the camera crew that brought back footage of the shelter bombing to New York, to NBC and CBS. Both networks, after initially expressing interest in broadcasting the material, then decided not to run it. Do you have any information on that?

I understand that, wasn't it the fellow who went with Ramsey Clark? Jon Alpert. Someone told me that he insisted on having his own commentary. I'm saying this without having talked to Alpert. One version I heard was that Alpert insisted on having a level of control which NBC wasn't prepared to give him, and some people think that maybe Alpert should have cut his losses and given them the footage and let them use it as they wished. I don't know. I wouldn't want to go further than that without knowing more about it.

DB: That tape is now making the rounds, as you probably know.

Yes, but the crucial moment when it should have gone on was a while back. I don't know whether Alpert did the right thing or not. I know some people think he behaved foolishly.

DB: What about environmental coverage of the war? There was much focus and attention on the tragic fate of the cormorants, for example, and the burning oil wells.

The cormorants obviously made an important photographic front page appearance. Meanwhile, there were very few questions raised about the ecological damage being done by bombing, about the fact that against international law they bombed the Tuwaitha nuclear research facility, and for weeks no one even asked if there been any release of radioactivity around there. I talked to Frank Barnaby, the guy who used to head up the Stockholm Institute for Peace Research, a nuclear physicist, who told me that the release potentially could have been three percent of that at Chernobyl, which was quite a lot. No one raised those questions. At the time, no one in the mainstream media that I know of was raising the point that, if you bomb the aquastructure of Iraq, you're going to end up with a lot of sick and dead children and old people, as you get the potential for disease. I wrote in *The Nation* at the start of the bombing war that it was germ warfare, in the context of the quote from Winston Churchill about how the British...

DB: They gassed the Kurds in the early 1920s.

They tried to do it from airplanes and technically they couldn't, although they bombed a lot of them to death. It was the birth of the Royal Air Force, because they were justifying the Royal Air Force on the grounds that it was a cheap way of controlling tribespeople. But the ground forces in Mesopotamia in 1920-1922 were using gas shells in their artillery. They were very keen on it. Churchill

thought it was a terrific idea. Churchill thought many
things like that.

But to your question about ecological damage. No
one raised any of these questions, at all. Bush was told
clearly by many people before the war began that the
Iraqis could fire up the oil wells, which is what they did
in the end in Kuwait. This was all ignored by Bush and
his commanders.

DB: One understands Britain's involvement in the
U.S.-led coalition, but what about the French? Why are
they so enthusiastically involved? What do they have to
get out of this war?

Although we're moving towards a multi-polar world,
the United States still has enormous clout and is still the
world's major capitalist power. I think a lot of economic
pressure can be and was exerted on France. The French
always play a double game—so do all countries, I don't
want to single out the French for this—they clearly made
their calculations, got the particular bribes that they
wanted, and then pushed ahead. I think the French Foreign Minister was eager to try to arrive at a negotiated
solution, and France saw opportunity that way. Finally,
when it didn't work out, they cut their losses. This should
be said against the fact that Saddam Hussein is the prime
person responsible for all these disasters that have be-
fallen the Iraqi people. What an idiot! What a criminal!
That should never be forgotten. I don't think most of the
Left did forget it. People like Fred Halliday in England
are now going around and saying the Left missed an
historic opportunity to brigade itself with Bush and come
out against Saddam Hussein, implying that much of the
American and British Left brigaded themselves with
Saddam Hussein. I think that's nonsense, self-serving on
the part of Halliday.

DB: Bush said in a March 1, 1991 press conference: "The country's solid. There isn't any antiwar movement out there. A couple of voices, but you can't hear them."

I did a lot of speaking in March and April, and a lot of the Left were shell-shocked and thought that they hadn't been able to do anything, there was a total collapse of the Left, and so forth. I think a lot of that was simply not true. They weren't realizing that the war was extremely short. The actual bombing war began on January 17 and ended at the end of February, which is about six weeks. The question is, how much can you mount in six weeks? There were those large demonstrations on January 19 and 26, but those had been in the process of organization since the late fall. It takes a long time to crank out big demonstrations. Actually, the more you look into it, the more you find there were substantial demonstrations around the country in late January. I think the level of resistance at places like I was in Texas A&M, which was until recently an all-male military school, which is where George Bush is going to locate the presidential library, by the way, and had the world's longest yellow ribbon, thirteen miles long—the little local newspaper was against the war all along. The more you find out, the more you find out there was a tremendous amount of resistance. A lot of what there was was effectively blotted out by the mainstream state-influenced or corporate media.

DB: How do you account for that 91 percent poll in support of Bush?

You have to remember what people have been led to believe. There was that Denver poll done by the people from Amherst, where they did a sample, tested people's levels of knowledge about the crisis, in late January or February. They asked questions like, "Did the United

States warn Iraq against invading Kuwait, saying that if it did so there'd be military consequences?" Most people said yes. Of course the opposite is true. "Does the United States normally rush to the aid of small beleaguered countries whose sovereign rights have been invaded?" The answer people gave was yes. Most people had a fairly idealistic vision of what the United States is up to, simply because they spend a lot of time glued to television sets which tell them that. The more you watch only TV, the more rubbish you tend to believe. So I think a lot of the 91 percent were people who thought the whole thing was a pretty honorable affair.

DB: How do you account for the seemingly substantial public support for military censorship of the media?

A lot of people don't like the media, quite rightly. I think many people hate the press, think it's disgusting, a bunch of elitists out to sabotage the national will. People instinctively hate the media, as we all know, partly for very sound reasons.

DB: Has there been a propaganda project to promote that notion?

Yes, occasionally politicians will have a whack at the press. These days they're fairly careful about it. The last people to have a consistent shot at the press were Agnew and Nixon. I don't think there's been much of an effort since then. But you can go into a conservative area and do a rap about the press, I remember doing it in West Texas, which is not an area noted for swarms of liberal ranchers, farmers and the like. Most of them will heartily applaud the stuff you say about the press. Then they'll suddenly come up with some right-wing populist ideas of their own to stick on the end. But a lot of the critiques ran side by side, at least for a while.

DB: You think there's some resentment toward the media, with people getting seven-figure salaries?

Of course there is. They look at someone like Dan Rather and Barbara Walters or these people and they know that they're paid two or three million dollars, Diane Sawyer and these people. They think they're overpaid elitists, and of course they're right. Of course there are yahoos out there whose analysis and general outlook on the world is pretty awful.

DB: Talk if you will about the lack of interest in the media about Iraqi casualties. For example, on June 3, 1991 in the *New York Times,* there's a front-page story that the Bush administration was distinctly uninterested in knowing the number of Iraqi casualties. What would account for the media's disinterest?

Uninterest, lack of interest. Have they been totally uninterested in the casualty rates? I suppose they have generally. Basic racism. I once did a calculus of how people regarded white North Americans and then Europeans and then you get towards Asians and the concept of number ceases to have much meaning. With Indians the basic idea is you get a horde without number, you can only think of them in units of about a hundred thousand at a go. In the case of Iraq, I think they quoted the Schwarzkopf estimate of the number of military dead. He said it went as high as a hundred thousand. Then the victims of the bombing...I was talking the other day about that to my brother, who's been back and forth to Iraq. He reckoned that the number of people killed directly by the bombing was around four thousand, a lot lower than many people on the Left are saying. I would tend to believe him. Of course, they'll never really know how many soldiers were killed. Some of them may have been buried by the bombing; other people deserted. It's very hard to get any kind of figure.

The Iraqi government is certainly not going to help. There is a real imprecision. Look at the lack of interest by the U.S. media on how many people were killed in Panama. They don't seem to have much interest in discussing the dead on the other side. It's still absolutely impossible to discover whether it was three hundred odd, as the U.S. military says, or up to four thousand, as some Panamanians say.

DB: Your new book, *Encounters with the Sphinx: Journeys of a Radical in Changing Times,* is coming out in the fall of 1991. Is it a collection of articles?

Not really. It's more like a diary which goes from the personal to the political. It is partly based on the death of my mother a couple of years ago and also about the whole changes with Eastern Europe. It's a journal about, as we call them, changing times.

DB: Is the work still meaningful for you? The lecturing, the writing, the phone interviews?

Of course it's meaningful for me. I wouldn't be doing it if it weren't meaningful for me. What a dumb question, Barsamian!

DB: People get into patterns, and you start doing something and it becomes rote after a while.

I don't find that. I'm enjoying myself more than ever, actually, doing what I do. I'm now doing a column a week for the *L.A. Times.*

DB: What happened to your column in the *Wall Street Journal?*

I did it for ten years. I used to do it one week and then Hodding Carter used to do it and Mike Gartner used to do it. After ten years, the *Journal* said they wanted to expand the pool and call it a day on the regular stuff. They wanted me to write once in a while. I don't think there was any dark mischief, I think they wanted to have a different mix on the page. I was glad to have had the platform as long as I did. I think many people sit there fuming and boiling with frustration and have no outlet for it. At least I can fume with rage when I look at some rubbish in the *New York Times* and then I can write a column about it in *The Nation* magazine or fume with rage at some idiotic thing Bush has done and be able to write a column about it in the *L.A. Times,* or natter away to inquisitive chaps like yourself.

Defense
against Thought Control

Becoming a Critical
Consumer of News

Erwin Knoll

April 15, 1991

DB: If, as you have suggested, the media tend to be milquetoasts and obsequious to state power, why did the Pentagon then need to go to such lengths to control the news from the Persian Gulf?

Because of the traditional and constant tension between reporters in the field who are trying to do their job and the corporate entities who employ them who are trying to keep everything under control and in line. A reporter who breaks a good story, a great story, will not be suppressed. It's going to break out. You've got to do it at the source. You've got to try and prevent the coverage from happening, because the next My Lai story, if one were to occur in the Persian Gulf, would get reported some way unless they kept reporters from being there to cover it. All of these horrible things that happened in Iraq during those 40 some days of the war were unwitnessed and therefore unreported. It's like the old conundrum about the tree that crashes in the forest: if nobody's there to hear it, it didn't make a noise. That's exactly the way it was.

DB: Why do you think the American public is willingly going along with Pentagon censorship?

My interest is in the number of people who don't go along, considering how thoroughly manipulated people are, by the education system, the mass media, by all the

185

organs and institutions that shape public attitudes in America. It's a wonder to me that as many people question it as do. I've gone through towns where every single mailbox and every single lamppost had a yellow ribbon fluttering from it. That constitutes tremendous pressure to conform. Who wants to encounter the wrath of his or her neighbors? And yet, amazingly enough, some people do and some people think things out for themselves and find alternate sources of information and engage in dialogue with fellow citizens on these issues. That's what amazes me, not the other way around.

DB: Other than *The Progressive* and other alternate journals and sources of information, was there any reporting in the corporate media the you would view as positive during the Gulf crisis and war?

Yes, there were occasional stories, but they were always rare enough to be remarkable. I remember, for example, that somebody on *Newsday* did a good piece on how the White House in Washington—this was in January, during the war—was doing a daily orchestration of the news just the way they did during the last presidential campaign. They would have a meeting every morning and decide what the line of the day was. You saw that played in the media because one day the line of the day was, for example, the horrible treatment of our prisoners of war by Saddam Hussein. Anybody in the Bush administration who talked to a reporter that day talked about that. So each day they would set up a menu of what to talk to the press about, and the press invariably responded. I said, hey, somebody from the New York newspaper *Newsday* actually did a good story on how that process worked, very revealing for the relatively small number of people who were lucky enough to read that story. There were other instances of that from time to time.

But there were also the opposite. I wrote a number of op-ed articles during the period in opposition to the war. They appeared in a number of major newspapers because I was about the only voice that they could find saying what I said. I played the role of the "token dissident" on their op-ed pages. One of the pieces appeared in one of America's half-dozen largest newspapers. I won't identify it because I don't want to get the man into trouble. But the day it appeared, the head of the Washington bureau of that newspaper called me up and said, "I'm so glad my paper printed it because I've been trying to say that on the op-ed page for the last few months and they tell me that they don't want me to say it be cause it would alienate my news sources here in Washington." So there are always people, even in the corporate media, who are anxious to do a conscientious job. But the corporate ground rules often get in the way.

DB: You appeared on the *MacNeil-Lehrer Report* five or six times.

Eight or nine.

DB: To what do you attribute that? That's relatively new, isn't it?

It started after the intervention in the Persian Gulf. I don't know, actually, what to attribute it to, but I do know that there's an outfit in New York called Fairness and Accuracy in Reporting (FAIR) which has been one of several organizations that have been severely critical of the *MacNeil-Lehrer* news hours being skewed so far to the right, for being so dominated by official spokespeople and conservative spokespeople. That criticism had been backed up by studies they did showing what kinds of guests they have on the program and where they come from and so on. Those folks at FAIR say, and I believe them, that my appearance on that show is a response to their criticism of it. So, in effect, I have become the "token dissident" on the *MacNeil-Lehrer* news hour. By appearing on that show, and I don't much enjoy this role, I sort of take the heat off them when they're criticized for never having anyone with my point of view on the program.

DB: I know the term "new world order" makes you shudder and tremble. What role do you see the media performing in that new world order?

They're going to be cheerleaders for it. They already have been, and they will continue to be. As bad as the corporate media are when it comes to matters of domestic policy—and they're pretty bad—that's nothing compared to the role they play in building this consensus, so-called, for foreign policy. That goes back to the years after World War II, the beginning of the Cold War, when a concerted effort was made in this country to put all criticism of U.S. foreign policy beyond the pale, make it intolerable for anyone to criticize U.S. foreign policy. That's when we began to hear clichés like "a bipartisan foreign policy," or "politics stops at the water's edge." It's absurd to say that. Why should these matters of life and death—and literally they are, not just for us, but for the whole world—not be part of the political discourse in America? Why shouldn't they be part of the public dialogue? But with the overt collusion of the Democrats and the Republicans and the mass media, we've built this notion of a broad national consensus where, whenever the government starts waving the flag or sending in the troops, all criticism is supposed to stop. Those of us who insist on continuing with criticism nonetheless are marginalized for the most part, pushed out there to the fringes, and told that our comments don't count, even that they're "un-American," and every effort is made to sustain that myth of a seamless web of support.

DB: You've presented a pretty gloomy picture of the American media as they function today. Other than subscribing to *The Progressive* magazine, what might people do to affect the media in a positive way?

Let's not dismiss subscribing to *The Progressive* magazine, which is a wonderful thing to do. I think the most important thing I would urge people to do is to be critical in their consumption of news from the media. Don't just let the news wash over you as if you're some sort of passive recipient of it. You don't have to subscribe to 30 esoteric foreign publications to find out what's really happening in the world. You don't have to have your own independent news sources. All you really need to do is start reading and watching and listening critically, intelligently, if you like, where you say to yourself every time: "Who's telling me this and why? What have they got to gain by saying it? How does it connect to what I was told yesterday? How does it connect with what I saw or heard or read somewhere else?" Once you start applying that process to the news, you'll be amazed at how much more insight you have.

You asked what we can do about the media. I'm not sure, besides improving our skills as consumers of an inadequate product. The media are not public institutions. They're not quasi-public institutions. They're private businesses. They exist to turn a buck. The simple fact is that they're not answerable to us in any way except to the extent that they need us as statistics when they go and sell advertising. So if you can figure out a way to hurt them in the pocketbook, which is where they live, then you can have some say. But if you're thinking that by writing in an intelligent and persuasive letter to the editor you're going to reform the media, no. In that sense they're unreformable.

My favorite analogy is shopping for groceries. You don't think of that supermarket as an institution for the advancement of human nutrition. You know what it is. It's a store, and it's there to turn a buck. So you read the labels and try to see what the ingredients are and what the prices are and you try to shop prudently. In exactly the same way, the morning newspaper, the evening newscast, they're not institutions for the advancement of human knowledge. They too are stores that are there to turn a buck. So you use them in the same prudent way. You try to analyze the contents and derive some nourishing information from what is inherently an unnourishing and perhaps even toxic product.

About the Contributors

Ben Bagdikian is the author of *The Media Monopoly*, published by Beacon Press. He is a recipient of the Pulitzer Prize and professor and dean emeritus of the School of Journalism of the University of California at Berkeley.

David Barsamian is an independent radio producer and journalist. His Alternative Radio programs are broadcast on public stations throughout the United States, Canada, Australia, New Zealand, and on international shortwave.

Noam Chomsky, long-time political activist, writer and professor of linguistics at MIT, is the author of numerous books and articles on U.S. foreign policy, international affairs and human rights. Among his books are *The Fateful Triangle, Turning the Tide, Pirates and Emperors, On Power and Ideology, The Chomsky Reader, The Culture of Terrorism, Manufacturing Consent* (with Edward S. Herman), *Necessary Illusions,* and *Deterring Democracy.*

Alexander Cockburn is a columnist for *The Nation.* He is the author of *Corruptions of Empire,* and *The Fate of the Forest: Developers, Destroyers and Defenders of the Amazon,* co-authored with Susanna Hecht. His most recent book is *Encounters with the Sphinx: Journeys of a Radical in Changing Times.*

Jeff Cohen is the Executive Director of FAIR, Fairness and Accuracy in Reporting. FAIR publishes *Extra,* a bi-monthly journal. Their address is: 130 W. 25th Street, New York 10001. FAIR's phone number is (212) 633-6700.

Mark Hertsgaard is an investigative journalist and author of *On Bended Knee: The Press and the Reagan Presidency.* His articles appear in *Rolling Stone, The New*

Yorker, and other journals and periodicals. He is a commentator on National Public Radio.

Erwin Knoll was a reporter and editor for the *Washington Post* from 1957 to 1963. Later he served as White House correspondent for the Newhouse Newspapers. Since 1973 he has been the editor of *The Progressive,* the country's oldest political monthly.

Michael Parenti, a distinguished political scientist, is the author of *Democracy for the Few, Power and the Powerless, Inventing Reality* and *The Sword and the Dollar.* His latest book is *Make Believe Media: The Politics of Entertainment.*

About Common Courage Press

Books for an Informed Democracy

Noam Chomsky once stated in *Necessary Illusions: Thought Control in Democratic Societies* that "Citizens of the democratic societies should undertake a course of intellectual self-defense to protect themselves from manipulation and control, and to lay the basis for more meaningful democracy." The mission of Common Courage Press is to publish books on the syllabus of this course.

To that end, Common Courage Press was founded in 1991 and publishes books for social justice on race, gender, feminism, economics, ecology, labor, and U.S. domestic and foreign policy issues. The Press seeks to provide analysis of problems from a range of perspectives and to aid activists and others in developing strategies for action.

You can reach us at:

Common Courage Press
P.O. Box 702
Monroe, ME 04951
207-525-0900

Send for a free catalog!